ADVANCE PRAISE

"I know of no poet who can tell a story like Marianne Peel. *Singing Is Praying Twice* is filled with pathos and empathy, populated with memorable characters who alternately amuse, enrage, puzzle, and pull at the heart. Taken together, these linked poems offer up a woman's life in all its complicated fullness, from childhood to motherhood and beyond. And running through and beneath these portraits, there is music—songs sung alone or with others, in unison or in parts, with instruments or unaccompanied, from polkas to lullabies, in sorrow or in joy. In this volume, Peel demonstrates, time and again, how 'singing is praying twice.'"

LAURA APOL

author of *A Fine Yellow Dust,* winner of the Midwest Book Award for Poetry, and Lansing, Michigan, poet laureate (2019–2021)

"In this haunting and deeply felt poetry book, Marianne Peel examines the toll of familial love. *Singing Is Praying Twice* gives voice to an intergenerational community of women who demand their places in the world. Within an emotionally fraught landscape, where children bend to the whims of their parents, and parents struggle to understand their children, Peel writes with the urgency of a truth-teller, sharing the details of a life lived with passion and pain, a place where no matter what happens, 'we carry each other home.'"

ERICA GOSS

Los Gatos, California, poet laureate emerita, author of *Night Court*

"Marianne Peel's *Singing Is Praying Twice* reads like a song that demands you dance! This book is full of the joy, and a little heartbreak, of lives well lived. Peel's characters are testaments to every stage of life, from memories of a mother's cigarette ash falling in a baby's face, to the anguish of miscarriages, to complicated connections within a large ethnic family, to the joys of an autistic daughter who asks, 'Mama, do you repeat something you want to remember one hundred times?' Throughout, you will hear Marianne Peel's wonderful singing voice."

MELVA SUE PRIDDY
author of *The Tillable Land* and finalist, 2022 Weatherford Award, Poetry

"The loss of innocence is the price we pay for experience, a realization nowhere more evident than in *Singing Is Praying Twice*. These poems are honest, and the lessons learned are hard lessons—a constant 'whipping what is more into what should be less' ('Ceremony'). In a dysfunctional world of unrestrained violence, chaos, and unholy paradoxes, we have no choice but to suffer the mistakes we were taught as a child…Yet there is always hope and an abiding faith that comes from raising four daughters, one of whom is autistic and each of whom must deal with their own unique problems as they mature and have children of their own. One grandchild, we learn from the narrator in 'Mapping Our Universe,' 'carries my name / into startling galaxies she creates. / We are ancient souls, the two of us. / Bright flickering lighthouse, / luminary just off the shore, / we carry each other home.'

"Forgiveness permeates these poems. There are meals prepared with love. There is music and dancing and song amid inescapable loss and regret. Therein lies the beauty of *Singing Is Praying Twice*, the loss of innocence is the price we pay not only for experience but also for salvation."

JAMES ALAN RILEY
author of *Uncertain Mythologies* and *Broken Frequencies* and recipient of the 2020 Thomas and Lillie D. Chaffin Award for Excellence in Appalachian Literature

"In these vivid, narrative poems, Marianne Peel is 'scuttling through the basement of memory' to make poems of family where domestic imagery sits comfortably with the iconography of patron saints, where parents, grandparents, siblings, and children are honestly rendered—an extended family full of secrets and joy. These frank and embodied portraits of ancestry and lineage are 'praise psalms' both beguiling and unforgettable."

MARIANNE WORTHINGTON
author of *The Girl Singer* and editor of *Still: The Journal*

SINGING IS PRAYING TWICE

Also by Marianne Peel

No Distance Between Us

SINGING IS PRAYING TWICE

MARIANNE PEEL | POEMS

Shadelandhouse
MODERN PRESS

LEXINGTON, KENTUCKY

A Shadelandhouse Modern Press book
Singing Is Praying Twice
poems
Copyright © 2024, Text by Marianne Peel
All rights reserved.

For information about permission to reproduce selections from this book, please direct inquiries to permissions@smpbooks.com, or
Permissions
Shadelandhouse Modern Press, LLC
P.O. Box 910913
Lexington, KY 40591

Published in the United States of America by:
Shadelandhouse Modern Press, LLC
Lexington, Kentucky
smpbooks.com

Printed in the United States of America
First edition 2024
Shadelandhouse, Shadelandhouse Modern Press,
and the logo are trademarks of
Shadelandhouse Modern Press, LLC.

ISBN: 978-1-945049-45-3
Library of Congress Control Number: Applied for

Cover Art: Marta Dorton, *Rhythmic Flow*, 2021, mixed media (including acrylic paint, gouache, pastels and crayon), 17" x 47" (used with artist's permission)

Cover art photo: Kevin Nance
(used with permission)
Cover and book design: iota books

for
Anne, Elena, Leona,
Alicia, Audrey, Annelise, Allegra
and Kate

CONTENTS

1.

Lessons from the Cellar and the Front Porch | 1
Huckleberries and Homebrewed Boilo | 4
Ancestry | 6
In the Afternoon, My Nana Smelled Like the Earth | 7
I Played Among the Talking Trees | 9
I Disappear in the Spiral | 10
Novitiate | 12
Blasphemy | 15
Hope | 16
I Once Saw My Baba Naked | 17
Full Moon Drum Circle | 19

2.

Black Lung | 23
My Mother Was Her Wedding Dress | 26
Honeymoon | 28
Belladonna | 30
This Is Real Music | 32
No Exception to the Rules | 35
Admission | 37
Scavengers | 38
Surfacing | 39
I Begged My Mother for a Doll | 41
Barbie and I Share the Same Birth Year: 1959 | 43
Ceremony | 45
After the Thunderstorm | 47
Wound | 50
My Ozzie and Harriet, Circa 1965 | 52
Priscilla, Fishnet Nylons, and Garters | 54

Mother and Child, 1968 | 56
Unsullied Weight of the House | 58

3.

Gestation Interrupted | 61
Soon, Mama, Soon | 62
Prayer to the Goddess Parvati
  in the Ambulance Ride to Ann Arbor | 64
Due Date Rhapsody | 66
Lamentation | 68
Fresh Market on Saturday | 69
Hospital Blood Draw Attempt, 11 p.m. | 70
Introduction to Art 101 | 71
In My Mother's Kitchen | 73
Dictionary Girl, They Call Her | 75
Notes to My Daughter, Who Happens to Be Autistic | 77
Dissolution of a Daughter | 79
Holding Hands with Strangers | 80
Accusation | 82
Severed | 83
A Loveliness of Ladybugs | 84
Behind the Curtain | 86
Liberation | 87
This Is Your Water Waltz | 89
Collateral Damage | 91
Mama, do you repeat something you want
  to remember one hundred times? | 93
Learning to Live 8.5 Hours from My Annelise | 96
I Cannot Tell Whether You Come
  from the Shadows or the Edge of the Sun | 98
Daughters, What I Want to Tell You | 100
Mapping Our Universe | 101

4.

Driving in Stocking Feet in Downriver Detroit | 105
Gone Missing | 108
Trying to Remember | 109
In the Driveway with Dad Before My Red Eye Out of Phoenix | 111
My Mother Doesn't Realize She's in Hospice | 113
Sacrifice | 115
When I Try to Talk to the Dead | 117
Incantation | 118
Midnight Novena in a Coal Mining Town | 120
Estate Sale I | 121
Estate Sale II | 122
I Am Still Waiting | 123
My Father Visits Her Grave Every Sunday | 124
Forgive Me, I Won't Call on Sundays Anymore | 126
The Color Is Always Never Blue | 128
Death Wish | 129

Acknowledgments | 133
Note of Gratitude | 137
About the Author | 139

On Children

    Your children are not your children.
    They are the sons and daughters of Life's longing for itself.
    They come through you but not from you,
    And though they are with you yet they belong not to you.

    You may give them your love but not your thoughts,
    For they have their own thoughts.
    You may house their bodies but not their souls,
    For their souls dwell in the house of tomorrow, which you cannot visit, not
          even in your dreams.
    You may strive to be like them, but seek not to make them like you.
    For life goes not backward nor tarries with yesterday.
    You are the bows from which your children as living arrows are sent forth.
    The archer sees the mark upon the *path* of the infinite, and He bends you
          with His might that His arrows may go swift and far.
    Let your bending in the archer's hand be for gladness;
    For even as He loves the arrow that flies, so He loves also the bow that is stable.

—Kahil Gibran
From *The Prophet*

SINGING IS PRAYING TWICE

1.

Warm huckleberries
collected in coffee cans
blue rust on your hands

LESSONS FROM THE CELLAR AND THE FRONT PORCH

    I.   I learned my fright of birds
the summer of 1967.

Mama sent me to the cellar
to fetch a mason jar of chowchow.
Vegetable mash of pickled cucumbers, reeking
of brine and caraway seed, sweet onions and mustard seeds.

Steep stairs narrower than my adolescent feet,
a dizzy errand descending the underground dark
until my fingers found the string hanging from a bare light bulb,
yanking in want of light.

And it was then they flew at me
a dozen chickens still alive and fresh from the market
all screeching and flapping and feathers flying
a flailing of beaks and claws.

Mama forgot to tell me she bartered for a dozen birds
from old man Rzemplinski. Got a price
she just couldn't pass up. Told me I could help
wring their necks for her chicken noodle soup
early Saturday morning.

I saved the feathers
I pulled out of my hair.
Ironed them flat between wax paper.
Slid the sheets in my cigar box treasures.

II.   Mama wouldn't allow no pads in the house.
Waste of good earnings, she said.
And when the blood came every twenty-seven days
I crafted my own sanitary napkins.

Sewed rags together with a delicate embroidery stitch.
Used whatever leftover colors I could find
in Mama's sewing basket. *You have the patience of Job,*
concentrating on those minute stitches, she used to say.

III.   Uncle Johnny played accordion after dinner,
out on the front porch. Bellows belching out
polkas and sing-a-longs from World War II.
Mama tapped her toes.
Midnight Dew Geranium nail polish
smeared onto her bunions.
She created an alto line,
always a third below the melody.

I would sit at Uncle Johnny's feet cross-legged
watch his right hand dance up and down
the vertical keyboard. Watch his left hand
move button to button churning out chords.
The air from the bellows
cooling my face.

IV.   Mama wouldn't allow no bras in the house.
Waste of hard-earned money, she would say.
So I'd bind my chest with rags,
rags smelling of pine and lye.

Wrap them round and round my chest
strapping my bosom in and down, persuading
my chest to flatness. Mama always told me,
You don't need no bra, anyway. You flat as a pancake.

   V. One night Mama said she was all tuckered out,
needed to lie down a spell. No front porch singing
tonight. Just me and the moonlight
and that song I couldn't stop singing in my head.

It's only a paper moon
swaying over a cardboard sea
but it wouldn't be make-believe
if you believed in me.

There was swaying and singing
just me and the moonlight
and this arc of song
erupting from my mouth.

My movement free and wild,
notes spinning from my lips
with an unbridled abandon
and my dancing just couldn't contain my bindings.

HUCKLEBERRIES AND HOMEBREWED BOILO

Her fingers always smelled of cabbage
when she made the *halupkis* on Saturday night.
She'd plunge her hands into that boiling water
slivering out the core of the cabbage,
unafraid of the blade.

I used to think her fingertips
must be callused hard
scalded beyond all sensation
the way she manhandled those cabbage leaves.

Her fingernails stubby squares, and I wondered
how she managed to wrap them around that bottle
of homebrewed boilo—
Boilo that burned my nose hairs when I took a whiff
Boilo that she slugged down between folding
the ground pork and sticky rice into a cabbage bundle,
raw pig in a blanket.

Long ago she was a young widow,
a dress-shirt presser. Her heavy steel iron
smoothed out the blood clots her husband hacked up.
Checks for the black lung came on the first of the month.
I used to find them, damp, in her apron pocket.

She told us *it's damn hard to fall asleep once he passed.*
She used to parcel her going to sleep
into measures of his wheezing.
She could count on that syncopation
to soothe her off to sleep.

She became an insomniac after he was dead and buried,
recycled his handkerchiefs into rags
   to polish the toaster,
   to spit shine her shoes,
   to dab at the lipstick oozing the corners of her mouth.

They found her one fine summer morning
when the mountain laurel was in bloom.
She'd gone picking huckleberries up the side of the mountain,
collected them in a rusted tin coffee can.

She used to like the sound of the berries clanging in that can.
Counted them till the sun made her dizzy
and she climbed back down the mountain.
Her old sundress, all covered in closing go-to-sleep flowers,
was hung on the bathroom door
over her acetate powder blue nightgown.

They found her in the bathtub all sunk down and comfortable.
A cigarette still burning on the edge of the tub.
A glass of boilo rippling through the bathwater.
Her fingers stained bluish purple,
the huckleberries still on her hands.

ANCESTRY

I seek out my blood, knowing
names have been truncated, squeezed out
like dungarees in an old wringer washer.
Ethnicity cleansed from each syllable. Obliterating
the Lithuanian out of root and stem.

My ancestors dug potatoes out of the earth.
Macerated them into bilini—potato pancakes—
grating them down to a nub of pulp. With more push
in the arm, there is blood in the bowl. A copper river
floating between the pulverized potato shards.

We fry these patties in crackling vegetable oil. Slather
them with sour cream. I choose the pancakes
with burnt edges. My Nana wants the ones blackened
in the center, where the gas stove performs its most efficient
work. My Aunt Bernice licks the lid of the sour cream.

When I stop long enough to examine my hands,
there is dirt imbedded in my palms. Soil trapped
under my fingernails. My hands smell of the earth,
damp and clotted. With hands that have labored
in stubborn fields for generations, I come to the table.

IN THE AFTERNOON, MY NANA SMELLED LIKE THE EARTH

Her shoulders were always burned.
We had smeared ourselves with baby oil infused with iodine
painting our skin a burnt orange deeper than the marigolds
planted in a circle to protect
the lettuce from the woodchucks.

She taught me how to thread
a frenetic worm onto a crooked hook.
Digging around in that coffee can tin
wet with dirt and the roots of the soil,
humid mud under her nails.

Sometimes trails streaked her cheeks
after she pushed her hair off her face.
In the afternoon she smelled
like the earth after the sun
went way, way down.

She taught me to cast my line
flinging her whole arm back past her shoulder
all in one calculated, measured motion.
The splash on the water should be quiet soft,
she told me, *so we don't scare the fish away.*

And then we waited.
Just the creak of the dock bouncing
in time with the water
moving all afternoon
bobbing us up and down.

Sometimes our toes would touch
splayed off the dock
and I would recite *this little piggy went to market*
just in my head because
we had to be silent soft, waiting for the fish.

She taught me to reel in, quickly,
but with no panic, no surprise, knowing
there would be only sunfish suspended from the hook—
little orange sunshines in our hands
on the dock every summer afternoon.

And she taught me to unhinge the mouth
to pull the mouth slowly from its worm feast
to toss it gently back into the water and watch it,
still hungry,
swim away.

I PLAYED AMONG THE TALKING TREES

One tree showed me how her leaves
were the double reed of the bassoon,
vibrating one against the other. Another
revealed how her tulip flowers
contained the bell of the French horn.
And another whispered how she kept her secrets
in the knothole at the base of her spine.
She invited me in, lifting me
into the pulp of her symphony. I curled
into this forest womb, spiraling in on myself.
Long into the night, she breathed her melodies into me.
Etudes on vines. Sonatas in buds. Concertos in the furl of leaves.
In the morning, I woke open-throated, pulsing with breath,
singing arias I learned in my sleep.

I DISAPPEAR IN THE SPIRAL

A decent where I lose all balance.
My dancer self has abandoned me
and each step staggers on a trapeze act
with a dilapidated safety net below.

Fishermen hurl nets out into the night
off the Bosphorus Bridge.
Tattered beards and tattered rags
held together with halibut knots.
They will catch nothing today,
not even bottom feeders.

The sea is as barren as my womb.
I cannot arabesque in this deluge
of quiet. I am waiting for the accordion man
to heave his bellows. Underwater
his tune gargles and spits out seaweed.

My legs snarl in green trappings.
A morass of algae stew,
a muddle of scum and kelp.
I summon a seahorse
to be my dancing partner.
We spasm and sprawl, legless,
a seizure of flailing arms.

She reaches for me, my palms up and open.
A two-step of a gesture. But I cannot hold on.
She swirls up toward moonbeams.
My shoulders press against coral,

my belly torn open
on the fringe
of a ragged rock.

NOVITIATE

There were nights when I wrenched wooden splinters
out of my knees. Always after days spent
straight-backed, no slouching permitted,
on the no-pad kneelers. Just raw
mahogany shards piercing my adolescent skin.

Penance for your sins, Sister Marie Charlene told me.

There were those late afternoons
when I would lie prostrate on the flag stone
face down, eyes pressed tight-shut,
arms perpendicular to my torso.
My body in the configuration of a crucifixion.

After Vespers, we practiced mea culpa. Always in trios,
echoing the Trinity. Sister breath-whispered her sins
to the shadow in the confessional. *Recount
your transgressions*, Sister Marie Charlene told me.
Mark them on your mind, like penetrating nails.

I practiced wearing a homemade nun's habit, hiding
my hair under the wimple. Wrapped my neck
in white cotton cloth. Draped rosary beads from my waist,
hung from a belt made of jute twine. Recited the Hail Mary
exactly ten times five. Glory be.

I officiated Mass in the garage. My blasphemous ritual.
My vagina shrouded beneath a burlap loin cloth. I offered
the neighborhood children broken vanilla wafers.
Placed crumbs on their outstretched tongues.

Sister Marie Charlene, early in her calling as a nun,
brayed and bucked at the vow of obedience.
To prove her submission as a novice Bride of Christ,
her Mother Superior instructed her to fail
her final exam. Purposely. As proof of her humility.

I longed to sail to the Congo with Sister Marie Charlene.
Wanted to minister compassionate kindness to lepers,
experiment with blood remedies: lamb's blood, canine blood
a ritual to drive out the impurity in lesions that devoured
the cartilage of the ear lobes
the tender flares of the nostrils
the calloused tips of digits
the whole hand, sometimes.
There would be baths
in the venom of cobras
in the excretions of climbing fish
in the two thousand doses of bee stings.
I yearned to be part of the cure. Prayer
halted the unraveling skin.

Walking through Congo villages at daybreak,
she breathed in the decay of tuberculosis,
now a shadow tenant in her lungs

In the end this nun's story was muted, broken.

Requesting dispensation from her vows,
Sister Marie Charlene donned the garb of a lay person.
Someone no longer of the cloth. She exited the convent
through the back door. Hair exposed to the sun and wind.

I walk with her to the train station, my hand in hers.
I sit next to her on the crowded car
and then on the boat that floats us far away.
We journey to a sanatorium with quiet light in the sunroom.

We sing duets layered with sacred text.
As we chant vespers in Latin
the evening stars gather
like an iridescent bouquet
in the night sky.
All is well.

BLASPHEMY

The way you tilt your left eyebrow
for emphasis. The way you laugh
in an octave higher than your speaking voice.

The way you assign your husband
the task of plucking your chin hairs
should you slide down into a nursing home.

Your husband becomes an expert esthetician
maneuvering the razor around
the mole just beneath your lower left lip.

You used to paint
a beauty mark on your right cheek
with the dull end of your eyebrow pencil.

You wanted to channel Marilyn Monroe. To sing
Happy Birthday to Jack Kennedy. To siren him
with song, while standing next to a framed photo of the Pope.

One night you wrap a string of rosary beads
around your thigh. A garter composed of pearls
and decomposed rose petals from Lourdes in France.

The next morning you check yourself
into the confessional booth.
Your delicate doily clenched in place,
bobby pins piercing your scalp.

HOPE

Green shoots like dew-hungry tongues
emerging from soft soot after a deliberate burn
of the forest floor

Aaron Copland's *Appalachian Spring*
when the flute and oboe vine their way
up a white picket fence on a bluegrass meadow

A white sheet clothes-pinned to a rope
hammocked between the birch
and the cottonwood

An aluminum tub murmuring
with hot water, Ivory soap
floating on the surface

A splash of pure vanilla extract
caressed behind my Baba's ears
before a Saturday night polka

I ONCE SAW MY BABA NAKED

through the bathroom door,
open a steamy crack.
Her hair usually pig-tailed
and tightened into a milky bun.
Now she is unbraided,
corkscrews of hair
scratching the back of her knees.

My Baba, an obbligato soprano,
almost a three-octave range.
Soloist in the Greek Orthodox choir loft.
She hums in Slovak as she stirs buttermilk
into yellow wax bean soup.

My mother told me my Baba listens
in heaven when I sing.
Cadenza woman,
I am in discord with the harps.
I cartwheel around the score,
somersault in this cacophony,
hoping I will never find my way
back to middle C.

On her piano, two keys stained
a bitter dark chocolate.
I lick those keys until my tongue
sprouts canker sores.
Carbuncles congregate on the insides of my mouth.
My teeth are explorers, wanting to burst them open.
Welts ooze holy water into my mouth.

I genuflect before the sheet music on the piano.
Mice stumble across strings.
No one has played this music machine in decades.
Not since Baba laid her Zehdee out in his brown tweed suit.

Neighbors came, balancing casseroles between oven mitts.
Casseroles like salve, like blessing.
And Baba let each one turn to rot
on the kitchen counter.
Nothing existed in her to lift them
onto the refrigerator shelves.
Nothing left in her to lower them
into the freezer, next to metal cans holding bacon grease.
The counter heavy with fermented cabbage,
a dustbin of shriveled scallions.
When the kitchen held all the Pyrex it could contain,
the casseroles lined the crooked path to the door.
Fatigued luminaries burning
with cream of mushroom soup and mushy peas,
chunks of Spam and clotted cheese.

Now I sit on the piano bench,
hands positioned for a minor scale
I no longer remember.
But Bach, I can play Bach for her.
That ordered repetition,
the necessary crescendo,
that cadence memorized
in the fugue of my fingers.
That, I can do.

FULL MOON DRUM CIRCLE

They say a band of white-haired women
will eventually take over,
pushing the suits and ties aside,
making room for Mother Earth's healing.
A click of the tongue,
instead of a lashing.
A desire to get on with the work
that must be done,
a willingness to speak truth
to twisted corrupt power.

The women will circle up
under the full moon
and by its dependable guiding light
the white-haired women will turn East
and braid each other's hair,
fingers weaving locks into plaits
strong enough to withstand winds from the north.

The women will drum
long past midnight,
palms connected to stretched hides
of deer and elk, of moose and buffalo,
fingers splayed
beating out rhythms,
calling everyone into the sanctuary
of their inner circle.

The women will drum,
composing a song of peaceful warriors,
ready to embrace the pulsating moon,
the stars who have gathered to eavesdrop,
the tree frogs who churn out the bass line
of this ancient melody.

The women will drum
until their pulses become one frequency,
until the solitary beats of their being
willingly and reverently
synchronize.

2.

So many strong hands
pressing dough into flatness
biscuits on the rise

BLACK LUNG

No one could find a handkerchief
that wasn't stained from his years of coughing.
A blend of soot and blood hacked up over the years
caused by the mines he couldn't help but breathe in
through his mouth, his nose, even his eyes.

Mahanoy City called it black lung, this coal miners' plague.
This coughing that kept wives up through the night.
Night, when it was worse because the lying down
made the miners feel like their own throats
would betray them, suffocate them.

Townsfolk called it black lung, this convulsing of the chest,
which eventually left wives alone in the bed.
A whole town of widows
who now collect black-lung payments
instead of their husbands' paychecks.

His kin laid Grandpa out on the kitchen table.
Had to put the holiday leaf back in
because he was six foot five, like my father.
Most families displayed their dead on the piano
but there was little music in this house.

Even the radio was busted from the night he'd had
too much boilo, that sticky homemade poison
in the brown bottle next to the garbage disposal.
I used to think this liquor ate Grandpa's throat,
pieces at a time, as he swallowed.

But it soothed Grandpa, for a time.
Made his throat numb to the spells of coughing,
the coal dust that always gathered in his throat and on his tongue.
He always smelled like dampness, leaving trails of soot
from his boot laces on Grandma's hand-scrubbed tile floors.

Hardly anybody came to see Grandpa,
all laid out in his best suit.
Neighbors feared him.
He wasn't a quiet drunk.
Grandpa was a dangerous drunk.

He took out his liquor on my grandma most times.
Always used the back of his hand
and Grandma learned to turn her head fast,
to never raise her arm to shield her face,
to move out of his path when he was full of boilo.

He used to hurt her things when he couldn't find her.
He'd take a whole box full of her housedresses,
set himself down
on the corner of Spruce and Second
and light himself a fire.

Grandma's dresses always had little blue or pink flowers,
like she was springtime all year long.
I watched the fabric flowers close,
shrivel up and die,
as he set fire to her cotton garden.

One time he laughed long into the night
until the six a.m. church bells rang

and he stumbled up from his cross-legged squat
and headed down to morning Mass,
making the sign of the cross on his sooty chest.

My grandma would scurry out
with that old metal dustpan
scrape up the ashes
throw them into the coal bin
this house always burned.

Then she'd have her morning cup of coffee
knowing the shirt factory whistle
would soon blow.
Softer than the church bells
but filled with greater demands.

Grandpa was a quiet corpse.
The mines had choked the life right out of him.
My grandma was quite a satisfied widow
knowing her dresses would now
bloom again.

MY MOTHER WAS HER WEDDING DRESS

A blazer and an A-line skirt. For decades
she boasted how she was so thin
the skirt had almost slipped off her waist during vows.

Her mother disapproved of this
dark-skinned Lithuanian she was marrying.
Of alcoholic stock. His uncles in the town paper

every Monday morning. Arson fire arrests.
They used to set torches to the garages
on the top of the mountain. Scared every damn pigeon away.

They used to burn the shoes of their wives
when they got liquored up. Whole town knew
they were howl-at-the-moon drunks.

My mother rented a post office box to hide
letters from her Lithuanian lover. Sent from Korea,
his Marine handwriting meticulous on airmail parchment.

Once her Marine came home alive, my mother
used to sneak out late at night. Would crawl
in and out of her bedroom window. Slide down

off the second-floor roof, hoping she didn't
bust an ankle or worse. Coming home, she'd hoist
herself through the front parlor window.

Her mother waited there, in the dark,
rosary twined in her fingers. As she climbed
through the window, her skirt inched above her knees.

With the divine power of praying hands,
her mother's black onyx ring
cracked down on her skull.

HONEYMOON

Listen. The banister is heavy
with a dead possum: no. The banister
is splintered by the heft of a racoon: yes.
Spiraled tail between its legs. Glassy eyed,
down-turned mouth. Paws splayed to climb.

This is a congregation of corrupted animals: no.
This is a tribunal of taxidermists: yes. Of men
in plaid shirts who know the burden
of ammunition in their pockets.
Whose hands corkscrew their way
through intestine and liver,
through spleen and spine. Is there a receptacle
for discarded parts? For abandoned shards of bone?
For remnants of gristle gathered along the fingernail beds?

The bride and groom inhabit a hotel
stuffed with dead animals. Eyes
like worry stones. Ears pricked alert
with the glue of embalming fluid.

This is the place of consummation. Sheets
will be inspected for first blood. The clerk
at the desk comes to attention at the ping
of the counter bell. He is counting teeth
that have escaped from the dead possum's mouth.
He clangs his fingers over an abacus.

Listen. The couple climbs the stairwell.
They maneuver around
the wet wing of a hawk,
the matted tail of a lemur,
the bloated abdomen of an otter
gone suddenly still.

The bride's veil,
now tattered tulle, snags
on the claw of an adolescent bear cub.
The groom's cummerbund
brushes against the belly
of a pregnant doe.

The clerk tenders the couple a roadkill cookbook.
There will be tripe in the morning's omelets,
blood in the gazpacho for brunch.

BELLADONNA

*"… I want to die with my high heels on,
still in action."*
   —Bette Davis

On rain days
I loiter outside the bathroom door
watching my mother
embellish her face
with pancake makeup.

She applies Nouveau Beige foundation.
Saunters her index finger
into the cervices. Corkscrews
her face from dissatisfaction
to admiration. Pats the doughy skin
of her forehead, unmarred
by asymmetrical lines.

She arranges her lips
into a Hollywood glamour pout,
embraces the vial of ruby-red amaryllis
lipstick, kisses the after-bath fog
on the mirror with ripe lips.

She paints an India ink mole
on her right upper lip. She imagines her dress
rising, exposing her knees and the lip of her garter
as she stands over a subway grate.

She coils her hair into ringlets,
bobby pins crisscrossed onto her scalp.
She tugs on each curl, suspending them one by one,
framing her face with sausage curls.
Weaves the dolphin-shaped flowers of the delphinium
into a crown. This wreath of larkspur,
toxic nectar on her fingers,
soaking in.

THIS IS REAL MUSIC

They used to call her Legs Gaydosh, my mama.
Had the hottest gams in her graduating class.
Used to roll up her skirt's waistband, revealing more and more.
Wore heels that paraded the curves of her muscular calves.
She sashayed to the whistles and hoots from the guys
hanging out in front of Truskowsky's Funeral Home.

My mother was the Polka Queen,
with her Fridays and Saturdays spent swinging
to "Pennsylvania Polka" and "In Heaven There Is No Beer."
Her dance card always filled, pimply-faced guys lining up
for a moment on the floor with her and that skirt that flared up
a little too high when she would spin.

But she married a hometown guy turned Marine.
Married him right after he returned from Korea.
Only story about the war anybody could coax out of him
was about him sitting on the picnic-style tables during meals
on the boat. How his tray slid down the table during turbulence,
how it came back to him with vomit from the guy three seats down.
A fellow soldier who couldn't bear the bucking of the boat,
whose gut just let loose
of prune juice and shit on a shingle.

Their marriage rehashed the same argument over and over again.
Happened every time they came home from a relative's wedding
or a shindig where music ruled the evening.
When the polka played, my mother would grab my father,
two handed, and tell him *now's the time*.

My father was a slow dancing man,
cutting the rug to only andante songs,
ones he could hum in my mother's ear.
She fancied him a romantic, a tender heart, the first time,
nuzzling in to the wordless tune he whispered
just for her.

But polkas are unrelenting,
and my mother's mind was made up.
Twenty years it's been, and you still won't polka with me.
Her feet were tired of his shuffling from side to side
and she longed to kick up her heels,
to sweat behind her knees.
At midnight, I heard my mother drop a record
 onto the living room turntable.
"Julida Polka," dialed up to a ten.
Come on. Just follow my lead.
This is real music. Be my 'Polka King' and twirl me around.

I heard the front door open, heard the screen door slam.
The engine turned over, and he was gone.
The record player kept spinning,
 completing the song.
And then the scratch of the needle
 rotating around and around at the end of the song.

I remember waiting up all night
 for Daddy to come home.
For his Chevy Impala to pull in the driveway.
All I heard was Mama's fingers moving
 from bead to bead on her rosary.
The scratchy needle punctuating each Hail Mary.

In the morning, Daddy returned.
He set a fluorescent pink box of donuts
on the counter,
pulled out the egg poacher,
greased up the saucers with butter,
and fixed us a breakfast of perfectly runny yolks.

Later, Mama cleared the table,
scraping at the dried yolks
with her best knife.
With the back of her hand,
she dislodged the colored sprinkles
from the frosted donuts.
Pushed them into the trash.
Like confetti, they landed
on the broken "Julida Polka" record.

Mama always admired a tidy kitchen.

NO EXCEPTION TO THE RULES

In the house on Roosevelt Street
bed inspection occurs at 0600 hours every morning.
Her former U.S. Marine Corp father examines the military corners:
taut triangle folded over and under.
A quarter tossed on the bed clothes.
If sheets are pulled tight enough,
the quarter dutifully bounces from bed to floor.

Next come the bathroom sinks. Mother's tour of duty.
To pass muster, the faucets must be polished.
No evidence of water droplets.
Bone dry, her mother says.

Kitchen next. Plates and glasses from breakfast
scrubbed and stacked
uniformly in the drainer.
Sink, too, *bone dry*.

Skirt next. With arms pressed flat against her sides,
her father examines the length of her skirt.
Hem required to be regulation length,
lower than her fingertips.

Shoes next. Spit shined with chamois cloth.
She can see her face
in her patent leather Mary Janes.
Cheeks scrubbed with pHisoderm.

The bus arrives.
Mr. Calhoun laying hard—just once—on the horn.

As she walks back to her seat,
she rolls the waistband of her skirt.
Once, twice, three times.
Revealing fresh scabs
and scarred playground knees
that take her everywhere
she isn't supposed to go.

ADMISSION

I remember my mother running down
to the racetrack. This mother who watches her son
flip head over heels over the handlebars. A *professional*
stunt master, minus the barrels or the line of cars to cruise over.
But my mother sees a ragdoll flopping through the air.
Remembers his bellybutton protrusion. Hernia baby.
No consolation from Czechoslovakian lullabies. Only liquor
rubbed on the gums soothes him. He is an alcoholic
by twelve weeks old. His burps reek
of whisky and scotch. He cries
for seven months, colic in his tears. Bone-tired,
my mother checks herself into the psychiatric unit. Stares out
the barred Detroit windows with unblinking glass eyes. Rocks
herself back and forth until she lullabies herself to sleep.

SCAVENGERS

They disappeared behind the flowers,
those bouquets stacked in the alley
behind the church. Funeral flowers
with banners declaring *mother* or *father*
or *beloved aunt*. The *daughter* spray
leaned against the dumpster,
like an exhausted prayer.

They had come, this mother and daughter,
to find a flower for her school picture.
Third grade. No money for the satin bows
from Rzemplinski's Five and Dime. Needed
the three chickens in the cellar for Sunday soup.
Needed the pork shank for bone broth on Monday.
Needed the sour cream for the Tuesday potato pancakes.
Mouths of thirteen children to feed.

Tried one shabby white gladiola
tucked behind her left ear. Tried
a lackluster yellow rose behind her right ear.
Settled on two bedraggled purple orchids, almost as big
as her head. With green florist wire, they entwined
the blossoms and vines into the arch of her pigtails.

And her mother wove a wreath of baby's breath.
Placed it on her daughter's head,
like a lopsided crown.

SURFACING

My father banned books in the house
when I turned fourteen. Thought I
squandered too much time entombed in books.
Novels peddling peculiar doctrines.
Dubbed me *Four Eyes*, my cat-eye glasses
sagging off my nose. Grabbed my chin with his fist,
slammed my mouth shut. Told me flies would
swoop in there, between my teeth. Would deposit
maggots on my tongue. He plucked
rotten potatoes from behind my ears, potatoes
pocked with grey eyes, murky cross-eyed pupils
shrouded in slumping skin.

At night I buried the back of my head
beneath the pillow, the embroidered case starched
and pressed stiff with my mother's flatiron. I shined
a flashlight on the book I'd scoundreled home:
Let the Hurricane Roar.

Wondered if my pillow
would asphyxiate my airway
in the cave of the night.

Wondered if strangulation
was possible
between chapters.

Wondered if I would drown
between pages. Interred
without a bell to wrench.

But with every cock crow
I woke.

I BEGGED MY MOTHER FOR A DOLL

A homemade doll, like the one
Tammy across the street cuddled.
And so my mother set out to work
with the tools she was given.

Uncle Johnny's faded yellow sock,
without a match in the drawer,
became her head and body. Still smelled
like the cherry tobacco he packed
into his mahogany pipe.

Her eyes became two mismatched buttons.
One from the overalls Zayde wore
when he burrowed down into the coal mines.
Another from the fox fur piece my mother
sashayed around her shoulder on special holidays.

My brother dubbed the doll *Frog Face*.
Weaponized her during a game
of Monkey in the Middle. I fought to secure her
in my arms.

Secretly I hoped she would unravel midair.
I wanted her to tear apart at the seams
while in flight. Wanted her cotton-ball stuffing
to explode onto the orange shag carpet.

I wanted to drown this doll of shame.

Pitch her headfirst into the bottom of the well.

Deliver her to the hognose snakes in the swamp.

Lurch her toward the croaking of toads.

Bury her under a pile of mildewed leaves.

I could not toss her in the Goodwill box.
She would slump on the shelf, alone.
No child would choose
this misshapen ragamuffin.

She is still in my memory box, surrounded by
monochrome photographs from a Brownie camera,
a box of my baby teeth,
a plastic bag stuffed with black threads:
stitches I saved from the time I flew
head over heels off my bike.
Chin busted wide open.

The doll is in good company.
Her mouth a round O of red corduroy,
perpetually open.
Forever startled and amazed.

BARBIE AND I SHARE THE SAME BIRTH YEAR: 1959

In fifth grade, we silently stared at the slide show
instructing us about menstruation. None of us
baptized yet with the blood. But Kathy had repeated
several grades, disappearing weeks at a time
for another cleft palette surgery. As we pumped our legs
on the swings, trying to touch our toes to the oak tree,
she told us I *started my period*. None of us
believed her fantastic lie. In the lavatory, right after recess,
she yanked up her skirt, tugged down her Tuesday underpants.
Showed us her bloodied pad.
She became our hero.

Before Easter that year, my mother dragged me shopping
for a resurrection dress, white gloves, a matching hat
with pastel ribbons, and a pair of white patent leather shoes.
Wanting a new dress, too, my mother instructed me
to zip her into a lemony dress two sizes too small. The heft
of her waist and hips, the way her flesh fell out of her bra.
The way she panted, then held her breath, instructing me to pull.
The zipper stuck at the mole in the center of her spine.
When I have my good girdle on, you'll be able to zip me in.
You'll see, she told me.

And that day, she fitted me for a padded bra, declaring
I was flat as a damned ironing board. Said I needed curves in the proper places to
attract boys.

Said I needed a girdle to flatten my pouch of a stomach.

Said I needed to dye my hair golden.
To rinse the dishwater blonde down the drain.

To be like Tammy, the girl next door,
the petite ballerina with a neck like a swan,
who lived on carrot sticks and cottage cheese,
on canned peaches and melba toast.

Barbie and I were birthed in the same year. For three bucks
you could own Barbie. Add her to your collection.
Slumber Party Barbie (1965) came with a pink bathroom scale set at 110 pounds.
She came with a book *How to Lose Weight*
with the advice "Don't Eat."

She received a belly button from Mattel forty-five years later.
As if a synthetic polymer mother of impossible proportions
churned her out of a plastic vagina.

Barbie's eyes came with a sideways glance,
a way of forever looking down
and away.

CEREMONY

It began with miniature bruises, really.
An index finger pressed hard
against the septum of the nose.
Determined pressure
to rid the face
of one bony protrusion.
Counting to one hundred ten times.
A perverted rosary prayer, nightly.
Without benefit of bead or crucifix
before disappearing into sleep.

Cuts followed later.
Innocuous little incisions,
if you must know,
in the places that had outgrown my bones.
Flesh that had grown too thick, sliced open.
A bloodletting
to flatten flesh to bone.
My clever knife
doing the labor of leeches
across abdomen, thighs, calves even.

The cat-o'-nine tails came later, to be honest,
whipping what is more into what should be less.
Beating down the desire
with faithful flagellation.
I admire my own fidelity
as the rhythmic stripes
play a kaleidoscope lament in my head
until the thrashing tool goes limp,
splotched with blood turned
gristle and gray.

Tonight I count my body.
One knee. Two knees. A pair.
One breast. Two breasts. A pair.
Clamp each shut tightly
keeping anything that could penetrate outside
at a secure distance.
I am guardian of this body.
And I sit here erect and silent
knowing where my bone begins,
where my flesh ends.

AFTER THE THUNDERSTORM

We neighborhood kids
would *caterwaul to high heaven,*
as my mother would say,
when the rains halted.

We knew my mother would be tending to the laundry.
Saturday chores. From hamper to wringer
washer. To the clothesline
with pillowcases and sheets and tablecloths
and daddy's boxers and my trainer bras
all suspended with clothespins. Our clean laundry
on display for the whole neighborhood to see.
The women would gather at the fence, where the four yards
converged. Gossip between slurps of steaming coffee.

We stole clothespins from my mother's cotton bag,
affixed playing cards
to the spokes of our two-wheelers.
Mine was a plain purple bike, with a pink
padded seat. Renee's was a banana-seat
bike, with silver and gold
variegated tassels suspended from the handles.
Her seat was plush velveteen yellow,
with extra padding. Even the pedals
sported neon lights. She glowed.
If I gave her a dime, she let me ride
her shiny vehicle around the cul-de-sac. Just once.
If I slipped her a quarter, she let me ride no-handed,
pretending I was a stunt master navigating a field
of oak barrels and discarded junkers.

But the best of times came after a thick rain,
when the storm sewers just couldn't handle the deluge.
The whole subdivision flooded, murky waters
oozing over curbs, over sidewalks, over
my father's manicured corner lot of sod, right up
to the sugar maple next to the front door.

A neighborhood of frantic parents admonished us,
warning us not to go near tainted water.

You'll catch encephalitis, Frankie's father shouted.

You'll contract typhoid fever, Patricia's mom, still in her petunia-
patterned apron, yelled.

You're sure to get salmonellosis,
howled Old Man McCormick.

But our rambunctious desire was more muscular
than their warnings. We plunged our bikes and our bodies
into this suburban surge. Drenched in all manner of
slime and sludge, we peddled.
The click-clack of the playing cards
created an underwater rhythm,
propelled us over curbs,
onto the easement of crabgrass,
making circle-eights on the groomed sod.

Nothing could deter us,
save the moment the streetlights came on.

And on those nights, we all received a thorough scrubbing.
We were scoured in tubs of chlorinated water—a kill-all for any rabid germs
under our nails, in our orifices, between our muddied toes.

We were tucked in, covers up to our chins, reminded
Sleep tight. Don't let the bedbugs bite,
our bodies spanking, sparkling clean.

WOUND

If all the lights in the house were turned out I could still feel the place where the blade severed my finger. I did not know the force of the blade. I was simply following instructions from the oldest boy in the neighborhood. In January '65, he piled snow up to the garage rooftop after the blizzard. The neighbors called him *a strapping young man*. I did not know what that meant at age five. He would tunnel a hole deep in the snow mountain. Told us *the devil lives down there*. This was an icy, frozen version of hell. No pitchforks or flesh seared by hot fire. Here you would be perpetually cold. He volunteered to push us all in. We embraced being afraid. It was what we did in his presence.

The summer of '65. I had never seen a push-reel mower. My daddy pumped his lawn-cutting machine with gasoline from Sunny's Sunoco. Filled up the red plastic container on Saturday mornings. Early. If I woke soon enough, I begged to go with him. He'd guide the silver nozzle into the container—and then let me hold the handle. The invisible gasoline surged into the container and the vapors made my nose and throat burn. But there would be our favorite frosted cakes afterward. As a treat. We'd take turns biting the ones with peanut butter frosting. Our hands full of crumbs. We'd both wipe our fingers on his coveralls. *Don't tell your mother* he would remind me. Our secret. I kept retasting the peanut butter on my lips all morning. Daddy had peanut butter stuck in his beard, right below his lip. When I kissed him goodnight, I could still taste that peanut butter.

But I had never seen a push-reel mower. When I asked the neighbor boy —so much older than me—he told me it operated by hand. By his hands. The splintered wooden handle lay on the crabgrass. This was a house without fertilizer. My daddy complained about how their weeds infiltrated our manured, manicured yard. How their crabgrass jumped between the chain link triangles of our shared fence.

The neighbor boy told me he'd show me how it worked, this motorless machine. *Bend down. Put your hand on the blade* he told me. All the neighborhood kids were there. Usually boisterous and darting between stalks of sunflowers and the Dutch elm that had died from plague, everyone was suddenly still.

I knew how to be seen and not heard. I used to eavesdrop at the kitchen door, hoping to hear the grownup gossip while drinking home-brewed boilo from the brown bottle stored next to the garbage disposal. When they saw me wedged at the door, they shifted to Lithuanian. I never heard the end of any story. Conflict always resolved in Lithuanian, secret code to my ears.

And so when the neighbor boy told me to put my hand on the blade, I did. I remember nothing moved at that moment—not the wind, not the leaves in the gutter. Even all breathing stopped. Never had this backyard been so quiet.

The neighbor boy bent over. Grabbed the wooden handle. Pulled it upright. I remember how tall he seemed, looking down at me. Looking down at all of us. We looked up to him. And then he shoved the hand mower forward, all in one determined push. The blades were set in motion—a flash so fast it made me dizzy. I saw steel and grass and dirt combine. A kaleidoscope of color that was brighter than the July sun. My finger churning, there between the blades, separate from the little girl watching all the colors converge. A rusty river in the summer crabgrass.

MY OZZIE AND HARRIET, CIRCA 1965

She'd meander down the stairs, small steel flask
engraved with her name in a loopy font
in her right hand. In her left arm, a wad
of soiled sheets.

*I like my sheets fresh and clean, soaked in
that blue bottle of softener that makes everything
smell like a maze of lavender. All purple in your nose.*

And she shivers. Asks if anyone wants a little
nip of warmth. *You know how I hate to drink
alone.* Offers to share her flask,
drowning in vodka and lemon-lime soda.

She unzips her duster of a robe, tells me
she wants to devour ice cubes. *Damn hot flashes.*
Wants to stick her whole head in the freezer.
Wants to lap up the frost that has accumulated
on the walls next to the frozen elk
and the twenty-six-year-old wedding cake topper.

She leans on the railing, pokes her head
through the bars. She shrinks into her
little girl voice, begging for a drinking buddy.
I'll be good. I promise.

My father grabs the wooden handle,
elevates his feet on the pop-out ottoman
of his orange-plaid reclining chair.

Devoured by a cumulous cloud of cherry tobacco,
he loosens the noose
of his thin paisley tie.

He slams the *Detroit Free Press open*, the spine
slicing his reclining body into a cross section
of Sunday comic strip characters:
a disowned heir and his blonde flapper wife,
a goof-off soldier and his sarge.

The newspaper crackles, puffs its ink
out and in. My father snores into
the news, his exhale decayed with possum
tail soup from a roadkill cookbook.

My mother falls onto the couch. I scoot
to the other end of the davenport. She is a bundle
of translucent nightgown, cold cream,
spit curls of crisscrossed bobby pins,
and a black sequined boa.

My mother has lost her house slippers.
Beddies, she calls them. Tells my wheezing father,
*my toes are freezing. I can never
get my feet warm.*

I hold my breath
as her bunions scrape
and scratch
my feet.

PRISCILLA, FISHNET NYLONS, AND GARTERS

My mama displays them on a mirrored tray,
right next to the Infant Jesus of Prague statue:
exotic bottles of iconic perfume
with the most alluring bouquets of fragrance.

A sensual harmony—rose and jasmine,
sour orange and sandalwood, yang-lang,
vetiver, vanilla and bourbon—
for nights with hair swept
into an updo and fishnet nylons
held up by garters.

She'd flounce that fox fur piece
sashayed around her shoulders,
with the triangle snout mouth
clasping onto the tail.

I used to dream that the fox
woke from the wardrobe of the dead.
Eyes pulsing, shaking off closet dust,
oozing formaldehyde from its ears.

I named the fox Priscilla,
after my aunt who owned a liquor license
and knew the preferred drink of every regular
who bellied up to the bar.

And then I would hear a gnawing sound,
knowing Pricilla was devouring her own tail.

When Mama came home,
I'd tell her about my dream,
how the fox had resurrected itself
from its taxidermy state.

She'd reassure me the fox was still dead, laying it in my lap.
Go ahead and pet her. I ran my fingers through the dead, dry fur,
avoiding the face, afraid
she would devour my fingers.

Then Mama asked me to dismantle her updo,
one bobby pin at a time. I counted
ninety-four bobby pins scattered in the sink.
Each one smothered
with bottled seduction.

MOTHER AND CHILD, 1968

Mama grabbed my hand and tugged me
to autumn picnics. Went up to the tar roof of our apartment
where huffing chimneys sputtered, the rooftop garden a tangle
of chokeberries and shriveling clematis vines.

Mama would lay down the blanket made of Papa's old neckties.
She'd tell me stories of each tie. The ones he wore to Sunday service.
Called them his *sacred ties*. How he always had a monogrammed handkerchief
in his lapel pocket. How his compression socks, stretched over his calves, matched his tie.

Mama doesn't go much to services since Papa passed.
Now, these autumn picnics are Mama's church.
A cabbage bigger than my head as the centerpiece.
Dandelion greens and cherry tomatoes. Ginger peach jam on Mama's biscuits.

Mama allowed me to scoop butter out of the crock. With my finger.
Once, she licked the butter off my chin,
threw her head way back and laughed.
Licked her lips with a smacking sound.

It was my idea to make clothes out of black plastic bags. I wanted
the wind to whistle into the bags, lift us up off that tar roof,
take us flying over the charcoal town. But we were rooted to this roof,
our feet planted solid, like the taproot of a burdock weed.

After the sun went way down, covered the dime store in shadows,
we'd toast each other with homemade bug juice from a wooden chalice.
We'd make raw potato sandwiches, smeared with mayonnaise and pepper,
on the heels of pumpernickel bread.

Mama and me, we stood there together,
her hand on my shoulder, admiring the stars
that illuminated the concrete, admiring the moon
that washed the everyday away.

UNSULLIED WEIGHT OF THE HOUSE

Mother's hands scurry through the junk drawer
searching for scissors. Dull blades. Yellow handles.

She corners me in the bathroom. Bends me over the sink,
my back presses over the edge. Cold laminated counter on my spine.

The room scrubbed with pine oil cleanser. The fumes dizzy me. Disorient me.
Blades brandish toward my bangs.

She has no level. No bowl to chop around. Just her cataract eyes,
blurred, to maneuver the shears. The room gyrates, spirals down.

I teeter. Muddied with vertigo. My mouth plugged with cotton balls.
My ears stuffed with cotton swabs. My eyes pressed shut.

I cry out. *I am going to faint. Disintegrate onto the linoleum.*
Cleanliness is next to godliness, she says. *We could eat off this floor.*

And then a surge of steel.
A blaze of blade.
And I am gone.

3.

Long before her birth
I touch my daughter's strong hand
arabesque of dawn

GESTATION INTERRUPTED

I dream at night
of the embryo inside me evolving
into a carnival oddity. An encephalitic head,
disjointed limbs, a gaping spine,
eyes spaced on the sides of the head.
Some bizarre version of a cockroach.

The fetus just forming, a Rorschach inkblot
in my womb. I wonder if I will bleed out
an ear, a thumb, or even a whole hand.

And then the bloodletting begins. That red deluge,
that slough on panties, seeping through jeans. Dead on arrival.

I try to decipher the hieroglyphic clots, knowing
they have dislodged themselves from some dark place inside me.
A broken wound on the wall of my prehistoric cave.

SOON, MAMA, SOON

Mama demands to know when the children will come,
when she can be called Beloved Baba or Babushka
when she can expect miniature handprints of flour on her apron,
making dough for pierogi with her grandbaby.

And I tell her, *Soon, Mama, soon* as she pats my stomach,
anticipating the rolling of a fetus beneath her palm.
Back home, always in the middle of the night the blood comes.
It comes every twenty-eight days.

My hands are raw white chalk from the bleach to scour the sheets,
to disappear this sloughing off of the inside of me.
Because this seed will not take root in me,
I work the soil with bare hands. I bury seed beneath fertile soil.

The vines of the zucchini nearly choke the tomato plants,
nearly strangle the corn stalks.
I have more than I can hold.
The root cellar is wallpapered with labeled mason jars.

Every shelf sagging with stewed tomatoes,
bread-and-butter pickles, cabbage-laden chowchow.
So I rent a wooden booth at the market,
price my wares lower than my neighbors.

On the way home, my wheelbarrow
stutters over ruts, jar against jar.
I wait for the crack of glass,
The commingling of beet and pickle juices.

I still have more than I can hold
and have become the village surpriser
depositing jars in doorways, on porches,
even in the hollows of trees.

Sometimes I sit on the curb the next day
watching boys and girls with playground hands
discover these food offerings. They run them up to their porch,
holding them precious to their chests.

They transfer these treasures to mother hands
emerging from behind screen doors.
I plant marigolds, too, and make bouquets
of flowers and vegetables.

A berserk bundle of garden in my hands
as an offering, to my mama,
for the child that refuses
to take root in the soil of me.

PRAYER TO THE GODDESS PARVATI IN THE AMBULANCE RIDE TO ANN ARBOR

Benevolent Mother Goddess of ten thousand names. Daughter of the Mountain. Remedy for everything present in the water. You used to pound clothes clean on rocks down by the river, present in the water carried up the mountain, jug balanced on a head level with the horizon, present in the bond that connects all beings. Lend me your arms and all you hold sacred in your four palms: prayer-beads, mirror, bell, and citron.

Steady my hands holding this intravenous line in place on this ambulance trek to Mott's Children's Hospital. I hold my daughter on this gurney. Side boards wedge me into place. I am told not to move. To hold still. Very still. To breathe with her around curves, over the potholes. Ease the jarring. Let there be no spaces between us.

Forgive me. All of her veins have collapsed. I presided over the ritual of every new line inserted. Every time they approached her four-pound body with needles and tubes. I could not abide an intravenous line into her scalp, into that last desperate place reserved when all veins have collapsed. Her veins are exhausted. And so I hold her on my chest in this ambulance, my hand pressed onto the dorsal arch vein of her hand, tethering her to the drip. A tentative connection. Unstable and wobbling.

I study the bruises on the backs of her hands, her wrists, the knuckle vein of her index finger, the tender places on her forearms. Failure to thrive: she uses more energy, burns more calories tying to consume the milk my breasts offer. Forgive me. Suckling daughter of mine, my milk serves only to wither your skin onto your bones.

And so, my dear Goddess Parvati, I grind your prayer beads in my teeth, splinter my tongue, swallow devotion slivers in my gut, muscle of fire in my belly. Ignite me. And so, benevolent Goddess Parvati, I place your mirror next to my daughter's mouth. Under her nose. Watching for the fog of breath, palpitation of inhaling and exhaling. Reassure me.

And so, my sweet Goddess Parvati, clang your bell once every mile. One traversed, another around the curve, each ring one mile closer to the saving place, that luminous hospital on the hill. Navigate me. And so, my healing Goddess Parvati, I have devoured the juice of your citron leaf. Pressed this salve onto my new mother lips. Sedative to uterine spasms, I bathe in this lemony-lime balm lingering in the hollow of my womb. Calm me.

Thank you, dear Goddess, for safe passage. For the gift of steady hands. I curl onto the windowsill of my daughter's room. But I will be awake all night long. There will be rocking and swaying. There will be prayer wheel singing and humming. Send me angels. Please. I am waiting by the door.

DUE DATE RHAPSODY
for my daughter

You are due today
and I want to place a butcher knife
beneath your mattress
to cut the pain, to turn away dark shadows,
to frighten off fear.

I want to rid your room
of knots, maleficent contortions
found in curtain cords and shoelaces.
Like the Greeks in Athena,
I want to untie the bundle of pain in your belly.

I want to lay you down gently
on a bed composed of animal fur
and knead your pregnant belly like the Zunis—
Zunis who birthed in silence,
with females gathered round, voicing groans and wails.

I want you to squat deep and low
over hot stones gathered by the Comanche
knowing the pain from the heat
helps prepare for the pain of labor,
helps stretch the perineum.

I want to summon a Taoist priest from Wushan Mountain
to whisper lamentations and prayers
into your infant's ears.
A guarantee the first words heard
are sacred and pure, blessed and genuine.

I want to place the placenta
in an earthenware jar from Malaysia
filled with green cardamom and coriander and star anise,
to keep the jar next to you for forty days
and then bury the jar beneath a blooming tulip tree.

I want to bathe your daughter
in oil and pink roses
and burgundy wine
as they did in France
in the sixteenth century.

It is said that a woman in childbirth
vacates her body and travels to the stars,
collecting a soul made of stardust and light.

And it is said that this mother
and this stardust soul
return to earth together
forever entwined,
never failing to illuminate
the lonely nighttime sky.

LAMENTATION

You have cried through the night for months.
Colic infant, no amount of boiled fennel seed siphoned
through a strainer will halt your wailing. I hold you upright,
minimize the air you swallow. I hold you skin to skin.
You bristle on my chest, contorting your mouth from one breast
to another. As if what liquid I have to offer
sours in your mouth, in the tunnel of your esophagus,
in the basement of your belly.

A tenant who hears your discontent night after night
tapes a note to my door: *take your baby*
for a car ride. The vibrations might woo her to sleep.
But I have no car. I barely have money for the acrylics,
for the blank canvases crying for paint.

You erupted from me with the cord coiled around your neck.
A silent birthing. A waiting for that first gulp of air.
For that first cry. But nothing. Your face blue
as the umbilical cord. A robin's egg blue that startled
even the midwife catching you in her palms.

I understand the mothers who try to shake their child
into silence. Who scream *stop* in the cave of their throats
and then try to shove the words back down their gullets.
I have held you over a balcony rail. Imagined just
dropping you to make the wailing cease. Letting you
slip out of my hands. A gentle thud
on the pavement.
All is quiet.
All is calm.
Everything laden with snow.

FRESH MARKET ON SATURDAY

The city is beautiful
and I have just been to the market.

My daughters tag along. Exquisite
pastel appendages. Brushed, polished, spit-shined.

They have just discovered their own hips,
the way a lopsided stance can speak sass.

Their hips make words irrelevant. They've mastered the slant eye,
chiseled me into mosaic fragments with their eye-rolling.

The butcher goes all teary-eyed
every time the bell tingles when they enter his stall.

Lace filigree around their collars. Patent leather Mary Janes.
Scissor-curled ribbons in their pigtails.

They are not ready to know how sausage is made,
not ready to see the goat head dangling behind the counter.

HOSPITAL BLOOD DRAW ATTEMPT, 11 P.M.

I offer to sit on her stomach,
to pin her to the gurney. She is hollow,
collarbone now like chicken wings protruding,
pulsing at me as she tells me *no needles, not needles.*

I show her my arm, prick it at the bend of my elbow,
prove to her how easy blood flows.
She curls away from the dripping vein,
fetuses up, with her face to the wall.

She wears a size two but chasms exist
between her sunken hips and the denim.
The emergency staff tells me *we can't force
a blood test on her.* She's a minor and they demand
only addicts or DWIs to give.

She swears if I insist the needle into her arm
she will escape to the bathroom,
vomit whatever she has consumed,
make herself sick. And it will be *all your fault.*

I pull the curtain between us,
creak it slowly across the track,
and watch my own blood dangle down my arm
and out of my hand.

INTRODUCTION TO ART 101

My first daughter journeyed out
of my womb wide-eyed, without tears.
All curious, surveying the world
on the axis of her neck.

Outside the ephemeral float of my womb,
this water baby birthed and puckered
with amniotic fluid.

Two days later, I bundle her
into a cloth carrier affixed
to my shrinking belly.
She curls in on herself,
this coiled miniature human,
at the base of this denim pouch.

At the East Lansing Art Fair, a wave
undulating as we stroll the gallery.
We gravitate toward the watercolors.
Monet imitations by the locals.

I lift her from the carrier. Hold her
in two palms. Give her the gifts
of lily pads and gardens of lilacs.
I narrate each painting, name the colors.
I teach her marmalade orange,
sangria red, sea serpent green,
jellyfish purple, black-eyed Susan yellow.

One day she will be the artist,
birthing blurred spring gardens
with watercolors, acrylics, even oils.
Circles will summon her on a full moon night:
halos, infinity rings, gears of wheels,
a khorovod Russian round dance, a wreath of bangles.
She pirouettes between heaven and earth,
navigates a labyrinth of carousels,
choreographs her own geometry.

IN MY MOTHER'S KITCHEN

A saucepan of canned creamed corn simmers
on the back burner at 5:30 a.m. Corn that will slather
the mashed potatoes for dinner. Before breakfast or lunch
is constructed, she asks me to chop. Hands me
a dull-bladed paring knife.

Wants the tomatoes in wedges, the radishes in circular slices,
the carrots in shreds, the cucumber in chunks with skin
still attached. The romaine ripped by hand.
Filigreed. She wants the salad layered, not tossed.
The glass bowl, not the wooden one.

This morning, I construct the salad. There are no spices
in this kitchen. Not even pepper or salt.

This morning, my two-year-old daughter tugs
at my shirt sleeves. Has a book in her hands. The one
about Geraldine and her blanket. She signs
please and then *more*, bringing her fingers together
telling me she wants to hear the story again.

I drop the paring knife on the counter, wipe my hands
on the towel hanging on the refrigerator handle,
and scoop my daughter into my lap.

She turns the pages right to left, wanting
to read the story backward. We begin at the end,
with the doll dressed in scraps of Geraldine's old blanket.
We end with the blanket whole, intact,
a full cloth with the border unworn. New.

And in the kitchen we hear a thumping sound. Dishrag
squeezed into a tight ball then slammed onto the counter.
Circular wiping, as if trying to eliminate
some toxic contaminant. Again, the balling up of rag,
the slamming down onto the counter.
Again, the determined scrubbing of Formica. She can never
get the counter clean enough. Sterilized enough.

I know this sound.
When the cleaning communicates her consternation.
She is a machination of elbow grease and fixed will.

I finally ask *What's wrong?*

She wipes the handle of the refrigerator
over and over. Strident strokes. I know she is ready to talk.

*How dare you allow a two-year-old to interrupt you. How dare you
let her disrupt your dinner prep.*

But my daughter is in my lap, signing *More*. She wants
to hear about Geraldine, how her blanket is saved
from the rag heap.

And so we sit together.
She wraps her own sock doll in a blanket.
Hugs it to her belly, to her chest.
Signs *More*. Wants to hear the story again.

My mother takes up the paring knife.
Begins to gouge the tomato, then reconsiders
and says to me, *You have work to do.*

DICTIONARY GIRL, THEY CALL HER

She is such a smart little girl. She doesn't daydream about butterfly wings or the color of the sea bottom. She doesn't hear elephant trunks bellowing in the clouds. She doesn't picture herself flying over tarred roofs balancing teacups on her shoulders. She doesn't use two pussy willow branches to ease her way down the mountain without scraping her knees. She doesn't climb trees, one knothole at a time, just to get to the top branch where the scrub jays squawk. She doesn't scoot her bottom across the cottonwood log suspended over the creek of belching frogs. She doesn't belly flop off the cliff's edge into the lake of flamingos and Fig Newtons.

She doesn't wear mismatched socks with her red plaid suspenders. She doesn't wear pink and white polka dot rubber wading boots to the park on a muddy August afternoon. She doesn't jump so high on the trampoline that her shorts split at the seams. She doesn't jitterbug outside in the thunderstorm without a umbrella. She doesn't unbraid her hair just to feel her fingers unravel the plaits. She doesn't unscrew the Oreo and ritual-eat the inside first, scraping the white cream off with her front teeth. She doesn't shove a Petoskey stone up her nose, just to see if it fits. She doesn't crack her knuckles just to hear the pops explode.

She doesn't slouch in the La-Z-Boy chair and eat Cracker Jacks out of the space between the cushions. She doesn't blow bubblegum so big that it explodes onto her cheeks. She doesn't pick at her knee scab just to see the color of the blood on her fingertips. She doesn't swim without a rubber cap, letting her hair sigh through the lake like a tangled web of moonbeams.

Right now she sits still as the sky. Dictionary Girl, they call her. She types rhyming words on the typewriter in her brain, calculating the syllables. She practices multiplication tables over and over in her head. She can't tell anyone that the 12s are hard. Really hard. Just too hard.

NOTES TO MY DAUGHTER, WHO HAPPENS TO BE AUTISTIC

     I.   You are three and have not spoken,
except for *minna minna minna*
over and over again.

I study sign language
for *mama, thank you,* and *please*
talking to you with my fingertips and words.

Paired like good wine and cheese
or peanut butter and jelly,
I invite you to come to this talking table.

     II.   In my every night dreams,
I brush my fingers under my chin, then under yours.
You follow my fingers with your eyes

And I see you mouth *thank you*
soundless communicating
with language on lips, minus the air to propel the words.

You sign *please*
and take my hand,
pulling me into a meadow

of blue petalled flowers
and baby's breath
under a full and vibrating moon.

You sign *dance*
and climb onto my feet,
swaying us in the moonlight.

III.   In our awake world,
I place the dusty contents of a Kool-Aid package
on your lips and mine.

I am inches from your face,
licking the Kool-Aid off my lips,
urging you to engage lips and tongue and teeth.

But your eyes are glassy and far away,
in a world I cannot see.
I pry a floor length mirror off the wall,

plop you in my lap,
face us toward the mirror
and lick my lips again,

making cooing, smacking sounds,
delighting in the gritty sweetness on my lips.
Your jaw is set and firm.

No amount of *mmmm good*
will convince you to taste your own lips.
You are wandering in a faraway place.

And so I hold you
close against my soft places,
singing *Minna Minna Minna*

along with you,
following your lead,
rocking to the rhythms you compose.

DISSOLUTION OF A DAUGHTER

She neglects to wipe the vomit from the underside of the toilet seat. She is unaware. Pieces of Sunday pork roast stick to the porcelain. She buries dead geraniums in her Baba's old hatbox. She blesses them with holy water she steals from the hand dipper at St Mary of the Sorrowful on Catalpa Street. The retired nuns blessed the liquid with a thousand Hail Marys. There are prayers breathing in the petals, incantations keening in the veins of the leaves.

The edges of her eyelashes are frayed. She twitches at them in her sleep. I find them on her pillowcase on Laundry Tuesdays. They are painted with violet mascara. They glow in the dark. I want to wrap myself around her. Slip my hands inside the woven basket that is her body. A waffle weave unravelling. I am punctured by her clavicle. Pricked by each rib bone.

Her umbilical scar is laced with pewter piercings, rings that rattle as she squirms and swims upstream. She ruptures between my fingers. She is unaware. I attempt to weave her braided sweetgrass self back together. My fingers clumsy gum glue. My hands birds-of-paradise trapped in cellophane.

HOLDING HANDS WITH STRANGERS

My daughters dredge all manner of relics
from the lake. Variegated seagull feathers.
Shell fragments with ancient rivulets. They long to find
a Coca-Cola bottle with a message wadded inside.

The lifeguard presses his lips
to his megaphone, bellowing out
an announcement. *Clear the water.*
Now. A child is missing.

I count my own daughters: one, two, three, four.
None of my own is at the bottom of the lake.
Mothers hug their sand-soaked children,
insist they *stay put* on the shore.

We know the drill. We link arms
as if we are about to sing *We Shall Overcome*
at a sixties peace rally. We form a human chain.

Our feet kaleidoscope the muck below.
We walk in unison, dragging our feet,
a marching band bereft of instruments
moving across a liquid field in slow motion.

The mother who has misplaced her child stands on the shore,
her hand across her mouth, pressing her scream down her throat.

I forgive you, mother, for blinking,
for that momentary moment
when your vision distracted
and your attention

drifted from your child.
When the heron bewitches your eye,
as she lifts out of the lake.
When the fisherman feels the tug,
reeling in a mackerel slick as soap.

We are shoulder to shoulder, a cotillion of concern.
We press our soles into the mud and the pebbles,
the sticks and twigs. We are a communion of agitators,
a human link of benevolence.

The silence stiffens the air.
The day has gone mute.

ACCUSATION

I don't recognize the crazed mother
I've become when they walk through the door.
No hugs or rushing to greet me. Those hellos
that used to knock me almost off my knees
with their giggling thrust into my arms are now so gone
and replaced with whispers between them confirming
it's all her fault, this monster who has rejected our father.
They know nothing of drowned passion
of rigid backs in the night of disembodied sex
drained of all intimacy. I left their father
because I couldn't pretend anymore. Because
behind the shut-tight eyes I was floating in a foreign land,
wandering, further and farther away, wrapped in my
exotic scarves, a watercolor of an artist's palette.

And when they walk through the door now
they drag in such acidic accusation. As if
I could remain false without my bones
fragmenting under my skin,
splintering my marrow. I cannot count the shards
that swim and slug beneath my skin.
They won't comply with the simplest of requests:
please wash your hands before dinner
please place your clean laundry in your drawers—
please brush your teeth
before going out into the world
becomes a battleground of feet
stomping up the stairs
seeking sanctuary behind slammed doors.

SEVERED

One night my daughter walked the midnight roads
surrounding Walloon Lake. No shoulder to ease
the footing. Just a drop off beyond the asphalt. Ditches
like open graves along Daggert Road. She tells me
of depression. Anxiety. She navigates her grief by mapping
her body with scars. The indentation in her belly
is my doing. The scar from the cut umbilical cord.
Separating her from me. I saved that cord stump.
Put it in an old Kodak film case. Remnant of the lifeline
connecting mother and daughter. Now one of many scars
etched along her attempts to negotiate her journey.
She has pierced her belly button.
Bedazzled rings of rhinestones
glitter at her very center.

A LOVELINESS OF LADYBUGS

There were days when she spoke in fragments,
in sentences minus verbs,
sometimes just a stammering of adjectives.

Is my daughter telling me
about trees or rocks or clouds?
Or the gravel path
that was just an idea of a road?

Her pockets filled with shriveled leaves
and lint. With orange berries
and pussy willow buds
smooth as a caterpillar.
Worry beads in her pocket.

Once I made a burgundy fleece robe
for her. Sewed strings into the pockets.
Something for her thumb and forefinger to twirl.
All that friction firing
just under her touch.

Last month she counted eleven ladybugs
on her windowsill. She worried,
if they got too close to the radiator,
their wings would melt.
She named one Icarus,
and all the others "I" names:
Isabella, Ingrid, Ivy, Iris, Imogene,
Irene, Ida, Ivanna, Ivory, and Iliana.

She turned the heat off for a week,
determined to protect this cluster
from the hiss and spit of the radiator.

They will bring me luck, she told me.

Last winter she found a brown house moth
clinging to her kitchen window.
She fed her with cotton balls
doused in sugar water. Flakes of oatmeal.

Nothing ever dies, she tells me,
if we tend to the business of living.

BEHIND THE CURTAIN

My daughter tells me all the girls do it:
stash those miniature liquor bottles
in their stilettos.
Gift-wrapped in taffeta and lace,
they pile into a wood-paneled station wagon,
their fairy tale carriage. They are Cinderellas
on prom night, hauling a picnic of Doritos
and Dewars onto the dance floor. A tangle of limbs
dry humping. She tells me the boys
bring an extra pair of underwear, just in case.

The smoking doors ooze with a labyrinth
of tuxedos and tulle. Cellophane cigarette wrappers
stick to the bottoms of their rented wingtips.
A Marlboro passes from one lipsticked lip
to another. Rouge Diabolique is all the rage
this season. They channel Marilyn Monroe,
with five coats slathered on pouts, with cleavage
exposed more than enough to tease, to titillate.
The girls stand over an open grate, kick
their heels up, watch their skirts parachute
higher and higher. Higher than their knees.
Higher than their thigh-high fishnet hose.

The girls smudge Channel No 5 behind
each other's ears, down the shank of their necks,
into the breadth between their breasts.

A migraine of smoke and ash wrangles
through pleated cummerbunds.

A string of broken pearls scatters on the dance floor.

LIBERATION

You, my daughter who refused a bra. You who wandered
into the boy's section at Sears. Hid in the dressing room
with a stiff pile of Husky denim jeans. Your thighs
like cords of firewood stacked behind the barn.
No amount of pulling or tugging could contain
those sturdy legs in swishy silk or red velveteen.

Didn't I tell you that you sucked on squares of flannel?
That you teethed on patches of corduroy? That your feet
stretched toward houses of wool?

You told me that three girls
at a fourth-grade sleepover
held you down.
Painted your toenails pink.

Years from now, you will sit on a high-top bar stool.
As you become bridesmaid for your sister's wedding,
the stylist will weave baby's breath in your braided hair.
Apply foundation. Line your eyes with purple shadow and kohl.
Extend your lashes with a wand.
Paint your mouth bright fuchsia.
In an off-the-shoulder dress, you stare straight ahead.
You refuse
to look in the mirror.

Years from now, you will shave your hair
down to a thick stubble. You will grab my hand.
Tell me to rummage my palm across your scalp.
And we will laugh together, watching the stubble rise and rise.
A life of its own.

Housed in a zippered plastic bag, you hand me your cut-off hair.
Tell me to donate these remnants to Locks of Love. Tell me
you just don't need them anymore.

THIS IS YOUR WATER WALTZ

I find you out back, beyond the fence, past the rock garden.
You have abandoned the shoreline in search of deeper waters.

Limbs like electric tentacles, you refuse to gauge waters with your toes.
You do not crawl or creep. You plunge face first into the opaque.

You temper your descent with your dancer's hands.
Your fingers swollen from rubber bands wound tight.

You have affixed your thumb to middle finger,
forcing your hands into ballerina hands.

I remember watching you press your fingers, like pincers,
into this choreographed prayer. Even in your sleep-dreams, dancing.

Jewels trickle off your toes as you move deeper.
Ornaments float to the surface.

You shed the lamb's wool that has cradled bloodied toes
forced into steel-point dancer's slippers.

You are determined to leave a trail of baubles and charms,
incantations to decorate the surface where you began.

There is a worm of blood swimming from your mouth.
Emerging from the center where your tongue bolt used to be.

A coming-of-age stigmata, self-inflicted, rising to the surface.
Breathing on its own. This blood offering, oozing from your open lips.

With a loop of gold, you have pierced your navel.
This indentation on your body, this visceral connection to me.

Singing you lullabies when I fed you in dark amniotic waters.
This piercing fragments your center, severs the cord.
This stabbing of your flesh, my flesh.
I watch you navigate your way to the firm ground of this watery floor.

Your eyes are open, even when submerged in water.
You breathe now with your pupils, irises dilated, vibrating.

A marine metronome. You are a trapeze underwater diver,
soaked in determination and your steady pulse.

I stand on the shore at midnight, tone deaf in this darkness.
I am mute, my feet sinking into sand.

You are all moon and fleshy star, a throbbing constellation.
You arabesque between starfish and seahorses.

COLLATERAL DAMAGE

A cormorant with a fishhook wedged in its beak
flails in Captain Gregory's hands. He pries open
this bird's mouth with pliers. Yanks out
the hook. Tosses the marauder back into the salty air.

Two pelicans, fish wire tangled in their legs,
squawk at the starboard side of the rig.
Captain Gregory grabs both of them
like conjoined twins. His pliers torque them apart.

I didn't know a seagull could steal shrimp bait
off a hook. I didn't know there would be
so many pelicans on the breakwater. I didn't know
the measuring numbers on the cooler decided the fish's fate.

Those too small— tossed back
into the rock of the wake. Those large enough
find a temporary home in the hull pocket of the boat.
A holding hatch.

I reel in a mackerel. Back on shore, I watch
the wide-eyed creature filleted, alive. Chum thrown
to the pelicans who congregate beneath the Fillet Station.
Captain Gregory pokes the eyes out. *Or else the head will float.*

At home, I unwrap the fish from the newsprint. Ink
has transferred to the scales, to the flesh. A classified
ad imprinted on its belly. Dealership hawking used Corvettes.
I could not handle the fish. Could not chop it up for tacos.

I leave the frying to my daughter. Show her where I keep
the Panko crumbs in the pantry. Hand her the real butter
laced with sea salt and olive oil. Slide the Cajun
blackening spice onto the counter.

I scour my hands with lemons. Scrub the acid into the cracks
of my palms. A blister is forming on the gash from reeling
her in. Flesh torn from a fishing wire is narrower – more
delicate - than any paper cut.

My daughter announces dinner is ready. Her face,
red from the sun on the ocean this morning. Her apron,
stained with fish flesh. She pushes her long, loose hair
out of her eyes with the back of her hand.

I bury my portion of the mackerel under shredded cabbage,
radishes, avocados, and aioli. Instead of tasting the fish
I concentrate on the scorching siracha in the sauce. Want it to blister
my tongue. Scar my lips. Want it to sear the roof of my mouth.

MAMA, DO YOU REPEAT SOMETHING YOU WANT TO REMEMBER ONE HUNDRED TIMES?

The passenger window rolled down,
I watch my daughter tumble out of the car,
approach the high school on her very last day.

There is no hesitation. Her hair bounces
long and loose down her back.
She navigates the world on tiptoes.

When she was five, after shaking her hair
all over her head, she told me, *My brain tells me
to slow down. Does your brain talk to you, Mama?*

My daughter refuses
to be defined. By labels. By doctors
who said she would never read. Never
write her name.

My daughter tells me
*I like the way the air feels
on my feet.*

My daughter enters
the Early On program at age three.
Yellow school bus arrives at 7:15.
She journeys to school with children
who negotiate the world on their own terms.
In braces. In wheelchairs. With breathing tubes.
Once seated on this truncated mini-bus, I cannot
see her. Her head disappears below the bus window.

How can I send someone
so small
off to school?

I want to follow her in my van. I want
to lurk in the rhododendron bushes outside
her classroom window, make sure she finds
her way down the hall to her classroom. Want
her teacher to greet her bounding self
with wide arms and an even wider heart.

This is my daughter who will learn to play
a plastic soprano recorder in fourth grade.
Ambidextrous, she seamlessly reverses hands
in the middle of a concert.

This is my daughter who will learn all the registers
of the clarinet. Will learn to wet the reed between
her lips. Will learn to cover the octave hole
with her thumb. Notes on the page an indecipherable blur
of staff and stem. She plays not by eye but by ear,
echoing her music stand partner.

This is my daughter who will run
cross-country. Emerge from the wooded trail
red-faced and arms pumping. Always the last
to reach her mark. Sometimes fifteen, twenty minutes
behind her teammates. They cluster around the finishing
banner. Cheer her on. She propels herself
across the line to a standing ovation.

I fear the world will not always be this kind
to my swishy-haired daughter bounding
through the schoolhouse doors.
Nothing will be the same after today.

LEARNING TO LIVE 8.5 HOURS FROM MY ANNELISE

The last time we talked
she said she wanted
every bone in her body
to break.

And so I picture her on a ledge
flirting with the idea of flying,
knowing she admires the flitting of butterflies
from phlox to sea holly to joe-pye weed.

I watch her wings
open and close, open and close,
like lungs rhythmically pushing
and tugging at the June air.

When she jumps off that ledge
she is one with the summer air
careening on currents,
her wings a blur of color

until she gently lands on my shoulder
all bones intact as she nuzzles my ear
humming that bedtime melody
I used to sing to her as an infant.
The one she recited in flawless Lithuanian
when she was twelve years old.

Years of sign language,
with me miming utterances
my fingers dancing words, whole sentences,
imploring her to speak

to say my name
to speak "mama"

but all she said for three years
was "minna minna minna."
Which meant nothing.
Which meant everything.

I hold her in my hands,
bones connected to bone,
this fragile flesh of my flesh.
This daughter who speaks
in the language of butterflies.

I CANNOT TELL WHETHER YOU COME FROM
THE SHADOWS OR THE EDGE OF THE SUN

A rhinestone stud in your left ear, you tell me
how you love to roam the fish market in Seattle.
How you carry a brocaded curtain around your shoulders.

How you sleep behind stall #42. The one with Old Man Clarence
and the one-eyed tabby. The feline who smells of day-old
salmon. How she licks your fingers with her raspy tongue.

How Clarence's fisherwoman wife barters with customers.
Apron pulled taut around her belly. Blood and salt coagulated
just beneath the outline of her breasts.

How you watch her carve out the most delicate bones. Pulling
whole vertebrates up and through the flesh. How the cat inches
its tongue between bones. Naked driftwood clean after her mouth.

You tell me how you abandon your body every night. Separate
from your body. How your body becomes meteor, flash of hot light.
How you circumscribe the moon, spinning on the axis of your spine.

You tell me how you become a seagull. On a current. Just
drifting. In an absence of fear. You speak
in the language of birds. Comprehending every guttural sound.

And you tell me how the fisherwoman always calls you back.
Connects you to flesh and sinew. Pulls you back from
blood clots that beat between the stars.

She sews you back together with pinpricks of light. Seamstress
of voyagers. Holy saint of those who wander. Needle deliberate.
Your seams secure. You are a rag doll of remembering.

The fisherwoman cradles you in her sturdy hands. Always
the remnants of fish flesh on her fingers. And she tucks you
into the curtain, these bedclothes you sling over your shoulder.

I want to travel with you on these night flights. I want to become
a lone blue heron. Primordial skeletal feet lifting through the sand.
I can only see out of the eyes on the side of my head. I want to be
the edge of the ocean, where algae blossoms bloom, fragmented
shells congregate. I want to take flight when shadows get too close.

I want to be a vibration in the wake of your flight. I want
to be the overtones that wake you, bend open your seams.
The seams the fisherwoman has etched down
the back of your calves, across the curve of your hips,
down your spine, across your lips.

DAUGHTERS, WHAT I WANT TO TELL YOU

You do not know
that even on winter nights
when icicles hang from the eaves
I push my bedroom window open
just a crack,
and I blow out the smoke.

There are nights that I want to play
In-A-Gadda-Da-Vida, Baby
or *For Emily, Whenever I May Find Her.*
Down in the basement's night psychedelic rock,
a kaleidoscope of rhythm and blues
of jazz and jive.

I am learning to inhale slowly.
Hold sweet Maryjane in my mouth,
swirl smoke like cabernet sauvignon,
feel my hard palate go slack
until my joints unhinge,
until my body unclenches muscle and bone.

I begin to float,
forsaking any stiffness.

Now, I can dance long and limber into the night,
hips swiveling to the tune in my head,
my song open to the nebulous currents,
the sighing of the wind,
the snow building on the windowsill.

MAPPING OUR UNIVERSE

I want to embrace the gravity of my body,
the necessary weight of each part, each act,
as vertebrae collapse,
shrinking half inch by half inch every year.

I have become soft.

I don't want to escape the brown spots
emerging on my hands.
Refuse to concoct disappearing potions
   of hydrogen peroxide and bicarbonate of soda
   of potato starch and sugar
   of apple cider vinegar and aloe vera on a cotton ball
   of citric acid and vitamin C from sour lemons.

I want my granddaughter,
the one who carries my name,
to connect these dots, these liver spots,
with a bright purple magic marker.
We are formed from the same stardust,
she and I, mapped from abundance
of oxygen and hydrogen,
a cornucopia of carbon and nitrogen,
a collision of calcium and phosphorus.

I want her to create constellations
on the tender surface of my animal body.
Primordial soup of the skies.
We are the infinite stuff of stars.

She carries my name
into startling galaxies she creates.
We are ancient souls, the two of us.
Bright flickering lighthouse,
luminary just off the shore,
we carry each other home.

4.

I bake oatmeal cake
my Nana's recipe card
smudged with sugar love

DRIVING IN STOCKING FEET IN DOWNRIVER DETROIT

My story begins with a phone call from my father
telling me my mother has run a red light.
And I picture her colliding with a maple tree,
whirlybird seeds dancing on her windshield.
A bumper crop traveling long distances
from the parent tree.

*Your mom crossed five lanes, her stocking feet
pressing the pedal to the floor. In lane six, a truck
t-boned her car.* And I imagine a steak medium rare
hanging off the precipice of a platter.
A Blue Plate Special pooled in its own bloody juices.
Not like the Wednesday night liver and onions.
No salt or pepper on the table. Just ketchup
to soften the leather of the liver. The gravy
transposed to burgundy as I squeeze Heinz
onto this organ slab.

My father tells me to come to the hospital.
She might be paralyzed. He told me the doctor said
something about her spinal cord being severed.
I cannot imagine my mother bedbound.
Can't imagine her in a wheelchair when polka music
traipses into the room. Her feet tapping relentlessly
to the dripping faucet,
to the woodpecker on the sweet gum tree
outside the kitchen window,
to the songs on the radio
she didn't even know.

My father has already been to the junkyard—
that graveyard where disfigured cars go.
The mechanic in him needs to see the car,
wants to assess the damage.
I picture the car draped in yellow-black caution tape.
Wrapped like a present. Wrapped like a crime scene.

Crushed, like a sardine can, he tells me.

He shows me the Polaroids of the Chevy Nova
in the hallway of Our Lady of Mercy Hospital.
I can't understand how she emerged
from that tangled mess of steel and chrome.
Funny thing. The license plate wasn't damaged, he says
as he pulls it out of the inside pocket of his jacket.
Of all the things to survive. A souvenir.

A nurse in a blue smock leads me to my mother's room.
She guides me by my elbow. Why doesn't she take my hand?
Just her fingers on my elbow, as if I am blind.

My mother lies as still and silent
as the soft pulsing of the night.
I search for breathing, wonder
if her chest still moves up and down
in the hospital bed.
She never nursed any of her babies.
I remember cigarette ash falling onto my face
as she plugged my mouth with a pacifier.
I could never catch her eyes. Those eyes.
Always looking above or beyond.
Always past me, searching,
as the smoke curlicued around her head.

My mother said, *I was thinking of you*
when I went through that red light.
Worried about you…and your problems.
My foot couldn't find the brake pedal.
I got confused.

And she lowered her eyes.
Asked for *more, please more,*
 morphine in her drip.

GONE MISSING

Once she disappeared
for three days and nights.

She has no recollection of where
she went. She knows she was profoundly alone.

No bourbon or gin, no rum or tequila
gushing in her internal tributaries.

No bender of liquor blackouts,
no spree of serial inebriation.

She couldn't find a pillow, her head
wedged into a crevice of concrete stairs.

She remembers bloodied cloths. Saturated
raw rags between her legs. Stuffed

into underwear. She kept changing
them out for dishcloths

for potholders with bulky seams,
for a flannel shirt torn into strips.

She remembers crumbling college-
ruled notebook paper to sop up the deluge,

wadded up love letters and lace
that she no longer needed or wanted.

TRYING TO REMEMBER

Now perhaps we are in a better position to understand. Seven years ago, she could not identify small spherical objects that appear on bushes, trees, shrubs. As if they no longer had a name. As if she had to invent what these round beings were. Sentient beings. With a life of their own. Separate from her.

People told her to relax. Let her mind go, and the word would magically come to her. Like rattling through a pantry filled with mason jars unlabeled. Cruel canner of peaches and pears. She holds the glass up to the cobwebbed light. Like scrounging through an attic on your knees, unraveling the rattan of the broken chair, taking dull scissors to the carpenter ants throttling the trestle of wood crisscrossing the beams. A blasphemous space to pray, in this place of cobwebs and creaks.

But nothing came to her. Letting her mind go conjured more anxiety. More not knowing. Others told her to concentrate really hard. Fix her mind on that round orange object. Connect the vision of that thing with certainties. With certainties she knew. Leaves. Stems. Petals. Roots. Dandelions cracking through the pavement concrete. She knew all the parts. But, damn. That orange round object no longer had a name or identity. It was voiceless. Tacit. Unwilling to reveal its own round-in-the-mouth name.

And so she concocted her own way to remember, scuttling through the basement of memory. She wanted to throttle names into revealing themselves. To seethe them into being through clenched teeth. She started with *a*. Produced all the *a* words she could generate. Seeing if any of them matched. Waiting for the round object to chime in, to speak up, to declare definitively T*his is what I am. This is who I am*. But that didn't work either. Just produced a permanent wrinkle in her forehead and a permanent grimace. As if Bell's palsy had taken control of her face.

She remembered that she had named all four of her daughters *a* names. Remembered running through a litany of names at the playground, when her daughters were like chimpanzees in rompers on the jungle gym, until she lighted on the correct name. And then she would conjure all the *b* words she knew. As if she were a walking dictionary. Then onto *c*. For twenty-six rounds. Twenty-six rotations. But nothing. Still no name for the round orange beings dangling off the bushes.

Trying to remember was like crocheting, really. How you try to turn a single skein of yarn into a blanket that steals away the cold. Lifts it off your skin. Like an infusion of light into your bedroom. Kick off the covers kind of light, heat. Warmth. It's that moment when you can close your eyes, coordinate the chaos of your fingers, and continue to loop the yarn into double crochets. Without even looking down at your hands. Everything becomes automatic. No counting. No need to think. To overthink. No need to give your hands more than a glance as you turn the corner, going from vertical to horizontal.

IN THE DRIVEWAY WITH DAD BEFORE MY RED EYE OUT OF PHOENIX

I need you to know that what your mom just told you, about making dinner last night, just isn't true. She hasn't made dinner in almost a year. Can't even put a bologna sandwich together, let alone a good meatloaf smeared with ketchup. Has forgotten how to make out checks. I'm worried. Worried that I will pass before she does. She just can't take care of herself anymore.

We're not eating much anymore. I can do poached eggs. Grilled cheese. But it's usually burnt. I can do tomato soup. I miss her stuffed cabbage. I don't let her anywhere near a knife. Afraid she'll cut herself up good. Coring a cabbage is just too hard. I been looking into nursing homes. You know, the kind that's an apartment with a pull cord. Just in case. Thought we could live there, like that, until she gets so bad I just can't take care of her no more. It's hard to wash her hair. I try to make sure she's clean and presentable. But sometimes she just wants to sleep. And changing her clothes, getting those shirts over her head or those pants over her legs is just too hard.

I know she'd like her fingernails painted. And I tried it once. Smeared that Sweetheart Red all over the tips of her fingers. Had to scrub it off with nail polish remover. My hands just shake too much. Most of the time your mother just sits. Falls asleep a lot during the day. Mixes up her days and nights. Wants to go out for pancakes at seven in the evening. One time she even took off all her clothes in the living room. Then she said she was ready to go out to eat. Took me forever to get her clothes back on her. She's better when I just give her the pain medicine when she asks for it. Sometimes, I try to slip her a half pill. But I know she's hurting and end up giving her the whole damn thing.

And that cookbook you brought me, the one you're holding in your hands. Just take that on home with you. You know damn well I won't use it. You know I don't read nothing but the newspaper. And these days I even fall asleep doing that. Thanks for the gift certificate to Red Lobster. She likes their stuffed flounder and those cheddar biscuits. She always orders a Manhattan or two when we go to Red Lobster. Says they soothe her nerves. Make her less jittery. And thanks for making her meatloaf recipe while you were here. I'll be enjoying cold meatloaf sandwiches with lots of ketchup. For the next couple nights. That's some good eating.

MY MOTHER DOESN'T REALIZE SHE'S IN HOSPICE

Last time I saw her,
she was scooping clam chowder
into her round Slovak face.
Occasionally looking up.
Giggling across the Red Lobster booth.
Three Manhattan glasses in a row,
licked clean. Only the curlicue stem of the cherry
as evidence.

Sepsis spreads through her blood
like a rollicking version of *The Clarinet Polka*,
the same music galloping
through our house on Sunday mornings
nudging us to wake up for services.
Now there is so much fluid around her heart,
drowning this pulsing muscle
as if it were an embryo
suspended in warm womb liquid.

Sixty years ago
the blood of a broken womb
spilled onto her underwear.
Always in the dark cave of the night.
Twice.

Now my father changes her Depends
every two hours. She awakens
in a bed of urine,
the stench of a catheter
that has come unhinged.

I want to remember my mother
with her face drunk-happy,
lingering at the edge
of that bowl of clam chowder.
Her mouth tingling with seriously hard bourbon
and the sweetness of vermouth.
Angostura bitters soaking into her gums,
orange peel wedged into the gap
between her two front teeth.

She never did learn how to tie a knot
in the stem of a maraschino cherry
with her now silent tongue.

SACRIFICE

I sit at the bottom of the well
writing a letter to my dead mother.

Telling her I searched for a piano.
Wanted to pound out minor chords
the day she died. A piano trampled with snow.
Blizzard on the strings. Middle C key stuck.
Maple syrup spilled on the upper octave.
Ivory stained with dark roast coffee
at the far reaches of my left hand.
The candelabra without candles.
Without incandescent tubes of light.
Like icicles dangling from eaves,
the glass crystals clatter in the wind.

Her red wool coat is draped across the piano bench.
The one she wore for twenty-two years.
So I could dance
in pointe shoes.
So I could play a solid silver flute
with open French holes and a low B-flat key.
So I could attend a singing and dancing camp
in the Pocono Mountains.

She showed me
how to sew a button onto fabric with this red coat.
How to scrape off frayed pilling,
fabric comb shaving fibers from the surface.
How to iron corduroy patches onto the elbows.
How to slip stitch the tears
in the seams of the black silk lining.

How to repair a drooping hem
with needlework that remained invisible
on the public face of the garment.
Everything underneath. Tidy.
And hidden.

When I heard she died,
I imagined her arms detaching.
Red wool coat sleeves floating
between the clotheslines in the backyard.
Fingers twitching at the cuffs.

I try to reattach her arms with clothespins.
But her arms have taken flight.

I remember her sitting next to me
at the Slovak church,
humming Gregorian chant.
Wearing that red wool coat.
With red lipstick. Buttoned up
to her neck with disintegrating wool.

Her coat fleece damp,
limp from the snow.
Fingers latticed into rosary beads,
she carries the alto line.
Compliment to my soprano.
Like incense floating
from note to note.

She always told me
*singing is praying twic*e.

WHEN I TRY TO TALK TO THE DEAD

The dead always haul out the tea set from the cupboard.
The tea set with the quilted tea cozy.
The dead sit with me around the tea table.

Sit with me low to the ground. I crisscross my legs.
The dead always straighten their legs. Stretch them
out under the coffee table. Sigh into eternal extending.

The dead have agile fingers. Fingers that can balance
a teacup in the palm of their hands.
Are infinitely ambidextrous.

They sip and slurp without regard for etiquette.
Sip and slurp with no decorum.
Satisfied guttural sounds.

The dead dance in my parlor. Dance
with limbs loose. A juke joint on Friday night.
Long after the factory whistle has blown.

The dead recite incantations. Lure me
into their vibrations. The vibrations that slow
the chime of the grandfather clock.

The dead sing me to sleep,
sing with melodies made of marjoram,
with harmonies made of steam escaping the teapot.

INCANTATION

      I.   The very last time I saw my mother
she was facing cinder blocks,
pounding her fists into the wall,
screaming for my father.

You hardly ever come to see me.
Why do you leave me at night?
Make it stop, damnit, make it stop.

Her catheter tube had come apart
from the elastic band around her thigh,
flailing now, slapping her gnarled varicose veins.
Her face to the wall, her back toward me.

      II.   Now she is ashes and dust
stored in an urn
my father purchased
from the funeral store.

He picked out one he thought she'd like:
a ceramic container painted
with blue cornflowers,
like her china set in the curio cabinet.

There is no fireplace mantle to display the urn.
I wonder if my father housed it on the kitchen counter
or placed it next to the statue of the Virgin Mary
or put it next to the painting of the bloodied St. Agatha.

III. I keep seeing my mother against that wall,
pulverizing it with arthritic knuckles.
Banging so hard
she shatters herself to ash.

Her silhouette lingers there, suspended.
All her molecules have turned to cinders and soot.

I put my ear to the outline,
running my cheek along where she used to be.
Hovering there above the bed,
she is a hive of dusty bees gone still.

MIDNIGHT NOVENA IN A COAL MINING TOWN

I want to tell you of my mother coming to me after death. How she stepped into the kitchen with her back turned to me. Always her back turned to me. Wiping the refrigerator handle until the stainless steel is raw. Polishing off the shine. Cleanliness is next to godliness. Gentleman Jack Daniels, her lover, stashed behind the electric fry pan. Trysts just after midnight. Adultery in a decanter. Accompanied by bologna sandwiches and Miracle Whip. Her mouth a vice of liquor and pickled olive loaf. She takes her booze straight up. Neat. No ice diluting the click in her head. Glorious click. She slurps with a straw drooping out of her glass.

And I want to tell you how she came to me as she slipped out the window with her back to me. That same window she snuck in and out of as a girl dating her Marine. The way her mother used to sit in the dark worrying over the worry beads praying bead after bead of rosary imploring the Blessed Virgin to escort her daughter home. Protective halo shimmering. Blessed protective aura. A hand extended to ferry her across any bridge. Damn the troll beneath, lurking. Nine nights with intention. Begging for intercession of Jude. Patron saint of desperate situations. A plea to Our Lady Undoer of Knots. Extend your merciful hand. Undo the knots that suffocate your children. And only to rap her daughter on the head with her black onyx ring. Hard. An oval shadow of a stone. Mama never knew what clobbered her from the silence of the dark. Just the sound of fingers moving bead to bead. Who would have seen this coming down on her skull. Warning signal. Trigger moment. The slow threading of fingers from bead to bead. Glory be.

ESTATE SALE I

My mother was not a costume jewelry
kind of woman.

My father dumps her glitter and bling
on the bed. I search through the pile.
Want to find my name
attached to a bracelet or a ring. Even
a sticker with my initials
on the back of a locket. Anything
to identify what she wants me to have.
Something she wore around her neck.
Something she slipped onto her wrist
before a night on the town, cutting the rug.
A ring she removed when gouging her hands
into the raw ground beef, flesh that would become
meatloaf sandwiches my father always ate, cold
wrapped in Wonder Bread and ketchup.

I hoped for a sweater,
the one draped over the kitchen chair.
Or a shawl.
Or a scarf she would batten down
with her mother-of-pearl broach.

But the jewelry is unmarked, and my father wants
to clear the clutter.

ESTATE SALE II

There is a tissue there on the dresser
dabbed with her lipstick.
My father has not thrown this
into the compactor. And I wonder
how he packed her housedresses for Goodwill.
Were they boxed and sealed
or wadded into a plastic bag?
Did he save a blouse to sleep with,
to tuck under his pillow, her Shalimar
lingering there, right beneath his face.
They slept in separate beds
for decades.

There are six button-down shirts
in my father's closet. Ironed
into starched edges.
The collar.
    The cuffs.
        The sleeves.
Hammered down with the weight of the iron.
He will not wear these shirts,
will not wash them, knowing this was her last act,
her last intention—ironing his shirts.

I AM STILL WAITING

Since my father buried
my mother's ashes
I haven't received any
acknowledgment of holidays.
No place markers of special events.
Not even a check, like my mother
used to write with factory-line precision.
She kept a ledger of checks, like a payroll clerk.
Balancing columns of monies sent in cards
from an all-occasion box
purchased at the dollar store.

Her only gift was a box
of autumn leaves.
*To remind you
of fall in Michigan*, the note said,
after I moved far away
to the oil fields of California.

I shared the leaves with my students:
the sooty burgundy, the burnt marmalade.
They had never seen a tree evolve into a fall bouquet.

I saved the leaves
in a shoebox from Hudson's department store
until they became miniature shards
blistering my hands with their acerbic edges,
until, housed in corrugated cardboard,
they became charcoal dust.

MY FATHER VISITS HER GRAVE EVERY SUNDAY

My father holds the urn, two handed,
and tells me of the cold
on my mother's lips
the last time he kissed her.

She always smelled of Camels
and Dentyne gum, Jack Daniels,
and midnight bologna sandwiches.
Her mouth a chronicle of food and vice.

Last week we selected the container
for my father's cremation.
A flimsy corrugated cardboard box, like a receptacle
to store winter sweaters under a bed.

My father shows me his name
on the gravestone, a 1934 birthdate
and a void after the dash. Limestone
waiting for his death year.

And I wonder who chisels these dates,
these berserk tattoos on rock.

There is a graveyard artist
smoking a cheap cigar
with a flask in the pocket
of his red plaid flannel shirt.

He scratches out a shallow groove
using a light hand.

Buffs and polishes
with beeswax and a rag,
a cloth doubling as his handkerchief,
monogrammed in swirly script.

His palms, creased with shovel dirt,
sprinkle holy water from the sanctuary.

He blows breath into the cove of his hands,
producing a smoky incense—
limestone dust from his lungs.

He is a proficient altar boy,
genuflects, eyes lowered,
and offers a toast with the bourbon from his flask.

Aged in new white oak barrels,
he drizzles the headstone with Kentucky liquor:
wood sugars caramelized and charred,
the gravestone properly christened.

FORGIVE ME, I WON'T CALL ON SUNDAYS ANYMORE

I was better off calling during halftime. But I didn't
know what game you were watching. Couldn't calculate
the hours lost between us. You in Mountain time.
Me in Eastern time.

You refused to mute. Not wanting to miss
a pass. An interception. The moment
when your guy crosses the line and flings his helmet
into the air. The moment the pigskin sails through the goalpost.

You are my mechanic father. Grease still in the cracks
of your palms. Grease still gathered under your nails.

To fill the silence during commercials, I tell
of the brake job at Midas. How I needed new pads and shoes.
How the car no longer pulls to the right or left after alignment.
How streaks on the windshield signal I need new blades
to see in the storm.

For years you handed the phone to mom. Afterward
she'd give you a Readers Digest version.
Condensed communication.

Now it is just us.

You pick up the phone,
ask *Marianne, who?*
I regret dialing.
Regret giving you
the opportunity
to not know

who
I am.

THE COLOR IS ALWAYS NEVER BLUE

The sky lives beneath my skin
simmering there like blue-tailed soup,
tubular oxen bones marrowed with turquoise stars.

Infinitely awake the sky sleepwalks,
an ambidextrous somnambulist juggling jester's bells,
an Appalachian creek troubling the veins of my waters.

Tonight the sky gallops under my skin.
Constellations of hooves,
galaxies of manes.
My mouth absent
of the bit. My teeth
unclenched to chant
praise psalms into milky ways.

I ride bareback naked
no reins in my hands
through a meadow
of sunset-orange poppies.

DEATH WISH

When I die, buy good chocolate.
One of those foot-long Toblerones
animated with hazelnuts. Break off a piece
every day for a month, until your tongue
memorizes the texture. Let me swim
in the sweet tastebuds on your tongue.
Line truffles infused with bourbon
on the edge of your plate. Taste
a morsel of the Kentucky I've slathered
onto my skin the past two decades.
Let the chocolate melt on the roof
of the words you have been whispering to me
as I lay dying.

Fetch a baguette from the nearest
boulangerie. Place it in an open paper bag
and peddle home with the bread
still warm in your bike basket.
Pretend you are in Paris, seeing
far too many paintings of Jesus at the Louvre.
Generous-spread real butter between the crusts.
Ladle honey from Greece onto its soft belly.
Play *Zorba the Greek* as you dance and devour.
Become the vibrating strings of the balalaika.

Gather the abundance of carbohydrates
hidden in red lentil coconut curry soup.
Slurp with a big spoon, the biggest spoon
you can find. Clink your glasses
on International Night, and toast each other
with wine from Argentina and pistachio baklava

from Woody's Oasis. Wrap your mouths
around Maamoul, date cookies from Syria.
Roll walnuts and poppy seeds into sour cream dough.
Create parcels of kolachi, Baba's Slovak confections.
Make angel wings and Aunt Bernice's prune cake.
Decorate each other's faces with powdered sugar.

Make chicken zigenfuss. Stuff the yeast dough
with full fat cream cheese. Scoop on the decadence
of gravy. Decorate with candied walnuts
and the white meat of scallions.

Compose a spanakopita galette. Layer the skin of phyllo dough
with melted butter. Stuff with feta cheese from Aldi.
Buy more than you think you need. Bake
on Nana's cookie sheet. Watch and wait
for the dough to succumb to browning,
for the spinach to sizzle. Lick the plate clean. Lick
your fingers. Abandon all etiquette. Indulge.

Then, plant perennials in my name: purple crown of snow crocus,
the laughing face of butterfly jonquil,
the bouquet of harlequin lilacs shedding softly on your table.
Wait for me to bloom, come spring.
I will return every April, and there will no longer
be any cruelness in that month for you.
I am your harbinger of spring.
Come, feast on the colors
I have left behind.

ACKNOWLEDGMENTS

"Ancestry"
    Highland Park Poetry (November 2021).

"Huckleberries and Homebrewed Boilo"
    Muddy River Poetry Review (Fall 2016).
    Jelly Bucket. 2018.

"In the Afternoon, My Nana Smelled Like the Earth"
    Silver Birch Press (July 2016).
    As It Ought To Be Magazine (August 2017).

"I Played Among the Talking Trees"
    Wild Word Magazine (Spring 2021).

"Full Moon Drum Circle"
    (as "Crone Manifesto") in *Gyroscope Review* (Fall 2020).
    (as "Prophesy") in *Innsaei Journal* (October 2020).

"Black Lung"
    Apricity Magazine (January 2017).

"Soon, Mama, Soon"
    Apricity Print Edition (May 2017).
    In a Clay Pot Magazine (Spring 2017).

"Prayer to the Goddess Parvati in the Ambulance Ride to Ann Arbor"
    ESME Journal (Empowering Solo Moms Everywhere) (Fall 2020).

"Due Date Rhapsody"
    Green Shoe Sanctuary (January 2022).

"Hospital Blood Draw Attempt, 11 p.m." (as "Hunger: A Poem in Two Parts")
    Ophelia's Mom (September 2001).

"In My Mother's Kitchen"
    Panoplyzine (Summer 2021).

"Dictionary Girl, They Call Her"
    Brave and Reckless (January 2022).

"Notes to My Daughter, Who Happens to Be Autistic"
    ESME Journal (Empowering Solo Moms Everywhere) (2016).
    Kaleidoscope: Exploring the Experience of Disability Through Literature and the Fine Arts (Winter/Spring 2020).

"Accusation"
    Apricity Magazine (January 2017).
    Common Chord Anthology (Fall 2019).

"This Is Real Music"
    Riverbend Review Art and Literary Magazine (Spring 2017).

Liberation
    Coming of Age Project Anthology (September 2021).

"Mama, do you repeat something you want to remember one hundred times?"
    ESME Journal (Empowering Solo Moms Everywhere) (Fall 2020).

"Learning to Live 8.5 Hours from My Annelise"
    Pulse: Voices from the Heart of Medicine Journal (2019).

"I Cannot Tell Whether You Come from the Shadows or the Edge of the Sun"
    Comstock Review (Winter 2022).

"Mapping Our Universe"
> *Coming of Age Project Anthology* (September 2021).
> *ESME Journal (Empowering Solo Moms Everywhere)* (Fall 2020.)
> *Gyroscope Review* (Fall 2020).

"Midnight Novena in a Coal Mining Town"
> *Literary Accents*, Volume 4 (Winter 2021).

"Forgive Me, I Won't Call on Sundays Anymore"
> *Muddy River Poetry Review* (Spring 2021).

NOTE OF GRATITUDE

It takes a village to be a poet. And I have such a gracious, loving village. A special thanks to Virginia Underwood, publisher, Shadelandhouse Modern Press, for believing in me for a second book. A special thanks to James Alan Riley, who was so instrumental as a mentor in redefining the shape and structure of this collection. Gratitude to The Coming of Age Project in Berea, facilitated by Libby Falk Jones and Jules Unsel, for being a safe experimental ground for new work. Thanks to the Wednesday Writers of Lexington: Shelda Hale, Marta Dorton, Jules Unsel, Kathleen Gregg, Laverne Zabielski, Linda Angelo, and Linda Bryant. I am grateful for many inspiring mentors: Erica Goss, Laura Van Prooyen, Jan Freeman, Leila Chatti, Katerina Stoykova, Pauletta Hansel, Marianne Worthington, Joyce Benvenuto, Laura Apol. Thanks to the daily folks in my world who give me honest feedback on raw drafts of poems I send them via text: Therese Wood, Patrick Lucas, Daphne Mitchell, Patricia Frank, Hope Nichols, Karma Vince, Jack Johnson, Michelee Spiers, Marie Kuzych, Diana Hrabowecki, Lisa Meadows, Joan Denton, and Susan Crosswait. Gratitude to my Wellfleet Poetry Group: Joan Mazza, Wilderness Sarchild, and Alyson Adler. Thanks, too, to my four daughters—Alicia, Audrey, Annelise, and Allegra—who have heard my stories so many times, and to my granddaughter Kate who has new and curious ears for old stories. And thank you to Scott Vander Ploeg, my beloved, who sits across from me as a fellow writer at coffee shops and is always willing to talk poetry.

ABOUT THE AUTHOR

MARIANNE PEEL is a poet, musician, and retired English teacher. She is the author of *No Distance Between Us* (Shadelandhouse Modern Press, 2021). She received Fulbright-Hays Program awards to further her research in Nepal and Turkey and to support her work as a teacher. She also served as an educator in China's Guizhou province and as a volunteer at Kara Tepe refugee camp in Lesvos, Greece. Her poetry has appeared in anthologies and numerous print and online journals.

www.ingramcontent.com/pod-product-compliance
Lightning Source LLC
Chambersburg PA
CBHW060527080526
44586CB00012B/645